The Lost Heritage

by

Walter E. Barton

DORRANCE & COMPANY • *Philadelphia and Ardmore, Pa.*

OTHER BOOKS BY THE AUTHOR

Federal Income, Estate and Gift Tax Laws (Correlated 1913-1953). John Byrne and Company, 1922, 1925; Callaghan and Company, 1938, 1944; Tax Law Publishing Company, 1950, 1953.

Renegotiation of Government Contracts. Bobbs Merrill Company, Inc., 1952.

Estate Planning Under the 1954 Code. Callaghan and Company, 1959.

Digest of United States Tax Laws. Martindale-Hubbell Law Directory, 1928-1940.

Fifty Years of Tax Law Practice. Dennis and Company, Inc., 1969.

Revision Editor, *Mertens Law of Federal Income Taxation,* vol. 7 ("Corporations"). Callaghan and Company, 1956.

To my Father and Mother

Contents

Foreword

This is a story that finds its source material in rural Indiana, between the Wabash and the Ohio Rivers. When one contrasts the setting of life in this Year Of Our Lord to that which prevailed in the Middle West in the pioneer days of nearly four score years ago, the transformation is almost unbelievable.

When the new century dawned, the log house erected by the great-grandfather of the author was still standing on the land. At the time of its erection, its setting was a new clearing in the forest primeval. Close by on the farm was the old log house where our narrator was born, a few years prior to the turn of the century. What is now a densely populated state was then a world without trains, planes, motor cars, or telephones—to say nothing of radio and television, which were to come decades later.

Instead of the isolation of the century's turn, there can now be seen and heard the happenings of the earth annexed to Main Street. When this story began, "twelve miles away" meant farther than are the ends of the earth today. There has come to pass literally a new heaven and a new earth in this brief span of one long lifetime.

And so in these succeeding chapters is woven a medley harking back to the days of the author's grandfather. It tells of log rollings, tree fellings, wheat threshings, mowings and reapings, hog killings, and four-wheel box wagons pulled by draft horses. There is a remembrance of dances in the hall above the nearest store, three miles away, with the rhythm of the fiddle accompanying waltzes and square dances—all to the tune of "Aunt Dina's Quilting Party—I Was Seeing Nellie Home."

We come across a country doctor hurrying, day or night, as he responds to any summons, riding to isolated houses, his conveyance not even a Ford Model T but a one-seated open-horse cart, or even horseback. A one-room schoolhouse stands miles away, the only transportation to it: two sturdy legs.

There is a remembrance of toil in the fields, from dawn to dusk, with summons to meals by the clanging of a bell or blowing of a conch-shell. There are glimpses of winter evenings spent around roaring fireplaces with the temperature below zero. There is the nearby barn with horses and cattle and the repeated, endless chores of milking. There are remembered baths in washtubs on Saturday nights. There are glass kerosene lamps, later superseded by metal gasoline lamps which gave a luminous, incandescent light—prophecy of Edison's miracle some day to revolutionize the entire world. There is a pungent smell of sawmills, and, of course, the country church served by untrained but devoted preachers.

In those vanished yesterdays is the gleam of fireflies on sultry summer nights, the cheery call of the whippoorwill echoing from twilight hours that will never return. There is the chummy croak of garrulous frogs in lily ponds.

The panorama displayed in those chapters of life stirs fond remembrance in the reader whose earthly pilgrimage goes back that far, like the scent of lavender and old lace.

But we have paused long enough in the vestibule. Let us enter the main building.

—Frederick Brown Harris
Former Chaplain, United States Senate

CHAPTER ONE

The Olden Days

SOME TIME AGO an old friend and I were talking about our boyhood days on the farm around the turn of the century and the incredible changes that have taken place since those golden days of youth. He was born in Central Ohio and I in Southwestern Indiana, not far from the junction of the Wabash and Ohio Rivers in what is sometimes called the "Pocket." Both of us have spent most of our adult life away from the farm, so, though of course we have heard of them, we have not witnessed the changes that have taken place in country life since we were young.

We recalled nostalgically the simplicity and serenity of country life in the Central West, when neither the federal nor the state government insinuated itself into the lives of the people. There was no income, gift or estate tax law, not to speak of the innumerable other laws and regulations, which are now commonplace. We had not reached the utopia where an individual could rely upon the government to do for him what he was unwilling or unable to do for himself. Emerson's philosophy of self-reliance was still in vogue, and one with ambition and will could find a way to advance, in spite of seemingly unsurmountable odds.

> There is a time in every man's education when he arrives at the conviction that envy is ignorance; that imitation is suicide; that he must take himself for better or worse as his portion; that though the wide universe is full of good, no kernel of nourishing corn can come to him but through his toil bestowed on that plot of ground which is given him to till.

1

"Have you visited your old home lately?" asked my friend.

"Only a few hurried trips during the years, but too brief to obtain any real insight into what country life is like today."

"Recently, I spent a week at the place of my birth, visiting a few old friends who have spent their lives there," he said.

"What did you find that was so different from farm life around the turn of the century?" I asked but almost wished he would not go into detail, for I feared most of the changes would be for the worse.

"Well, the most astonishing changes were in the methods of farming, the improvements in home and school, and the way country folk have been liberated from the soil."

"So you feel that your visit was rewarding as well as full of surprises?" I asked, heartened by his response.

"It certainly was. Why not take time off, as I have done, and find out whether you will know your old place when you see it? I wager you will find many surprising conditions, just as I did."

I decided that a personal pilgrimage to the banks of the Wabash and Ohio might be worthwhile. In the twilight of one's memory, to wait much longer might be too late. Next spring seemed to be the best time to roam over the old farm and to visit venerable neighbors who might still be around.

After this conversation with my friend, I spent several weeks ruminating over the "days of the lost sunshine," recalling the venerable log house overlooking the Big Creek Bottoms, the country home with its panoramic view of rolling hills and pleasant valleys. I recalled clearing the woodland, sowing, harvesting and threshing the grain; I pictured the one-room schoolhouse and church house, the village, the county seat, the early communistic community of New Harmony, and Lincoln's nearby Indiana home. Country customs and habits, and other well-nigh forgotten places and events of long bygone days began to come back more clearly than they had in years.

The years are bound to take their toll from one's memory of the distant past, so undoubtedly some of the radiance of the early days has been lost in the mists. With this tribute to Father Time, the days

2

in the country along the banks of the Wabash and the Ohio around the turn of the century will be depicted as clearly as they are projected to me through the vista of the years.

So, if the reader will linger with me and permit me to act as guide to the past, insofar as my recollection goes, these reminiscences may awaken slumbering memories in some of my contemporaries and stimulate an interest in others who have made their entrance more recently onto the stage.

> Oft in the stilly night
> 'Ere slumber's chain has bound me,
> Fond memory brings the light
> Of other days around me;
> The smiles, the tears
> Of boyhood years,
> The words of love then spoken;
> The eyes that shone,
> Now dimm'd and gone,
> The cheerful hearts now broken.
>
> —*Thomas Moore*

CHAPTER TWO

The Ancestral Home

SAMUEL BARTON, my paternal great-grandfather, migrated from Cynthiana, Kentucky, to Indiana Territory in 1815, settling between the azure Ohio and pearly Wabash rivers in what is now Posey County. A few years before, the southwestern part of Indiana had been opened to settlement as a result of a treaty with the Delaware Indians in 1804. In this treaty they ceded their lands north of the Ohio River to the United States. The cession was assured by the victory of General William Henry Harrison over the Shawnees at the Battle of Tippecanoe in 1811 and by their final defeat at the Battle of the Thames in 1813, at which Tecumseh, their famous chief, was killed.

In 1815, the western frontier ran along the Wabash River. Most of Posey County was then covered with a primeval forest of oak, poplar, sycamore, ash, elm, willow, sugar maple, dogwood, sweetgum, hickory, walnut, beech and pecan trees. They grew luxuriantly in considerable density and some at an enormous height. An early traveller reported that he had measured an oak twenty-four feet in circumference four feet above the ground, and that some of the trees were still larger. The county was far enough south for canebrakes and cypresses to grow in the swampy places along the lakes and rivers.

The forests were overrun with 'coons, 'possums, squirrels, skunks, deer, bear, wolves, wildcats, panthers, wild turkeys, grouse and quail. Parakeets, with grass-green feathers interspersed with orange and yellow, flitted about in profusion. Wild ducks and geese, anhingas and trumpeter swans frequented what is now known as Hovey's Lake and the Wabash and Ohio rivers.

Before he could eke out a livelihood for his family, it was necessary for my great-grandfather to clear a part of the forest and to build a log house. He and other pioneers cooperated in work, as well as in cutting tortuous roads through the primitive woods for their horses and wagons. In due course they obtained land patents from the United States, at a cost of $1.25 per acre, payable in installments—an amount of cash not every thrifty pioneer could manage in a single payment.

Flatboats were the only means of transportation between Southwestern Indiana and other parts of the country, other than horseback and wagon. It was in 1859 that the first iron horse made its appearance in Posey County. This was after my great-grandfather's death and during the 51st year of my grandfather, William Bradford Barton.

It is difficult for a person born into an affluent, technological world of plenty to conceive of the physical and mental hardships the early pioneers suffered day after day, year after year, with little relief. They had to clear the land, build their log cabins in the wilderness, cut new roads through primeval forests, and protect themselves against hostile attacks by the Indians and occasional onsets by wild animals. They made most of their clothes and grew their own food, except that furnished by the forests, such as wild fruit and wild game.

When sickness came, the pioneers usually had to rely on home remedies, as doctors were few and far between. When the Grim Reaper claimed his toll, they cut down a tree, ripsawed it into planks, and used the boards to make a box in which to bury their dead. Despite these hardships, some lived to the ripe old age of 100 years and were far more self-sufficient than their grandchildren might believe.

My grandfather, who was seven years of age when my great-grandfather settled in Southwestern Indiana, inherited some of the land from his father and added to his holdings, until he owned about 200 acres. He lived in the log house which his father had built on his acreage, situated at the top of a long hill sloping toward the north. Big Creek could be seen from this vantage point, slowly meandering southwestwardly to the Wabash. By the time I arrived on the scene, most of his land had been cleared. The farm was about half hill and half bottom land. When Big Creek overflowed its banks, the floodwaters deposited a rich alluvium on the lowlands, which made the ground fertile for the growing of crops, especially corn.

My father, Anson Barton, was born in the ancestral log house in 1861, and I arrived in a log cabin built at the foot of the hill several years before the turn of the century.

In 1892, my grandfather was interred in the community graveyard on his farm. Most rural burial places at that time were a part of the country churchyard. Some, however, were located on farms, when distances to a church were too great, or when it was felt that the deceased truly belonged in spirit to the place where he had lived and worked for so many years.

During the year of my grandfather's death, my father bought an adjacent farm and, somewhat later, an acreage in the Big Creek Bottoms at an average cost of around $25.00 per acre. This was a princely price then—but few things were more esteemed by a farmer than his land.

After the death of my grandfather, Grandmother and her son Tom continued to live in the old log house and to farm the land.

Our new home and Grandmother's house were about a mile apart. To visit her, it was necessary to take a public dirt road to the graveyard, then to walk along a private lane which skirted it along the north and meandered through the woods to her house several hundred yards beyond.

Frequently, I went to Grandmother's house at night. Often, as I was passing the cemetery, on hearing the lamentations of the owls wailing in the nearby woods and seeing the fantastic shadows of the leafy branches flitting over the tombstones, making evanescent frescoes in the moonlight, visions of ghosts flashed through my head, my hair stood on end, and my feet seemed to tread on air, as

I sped along the winding path to Grandmother's house. Belief in "spooks" was no laughing matter in the countryside around the turn of the century.

The old log house was built during the first quarter of the nineteenth century, shortly after my great-grandfather migrated from Kentucky. It had three large rooms protected on the south side by a long covered porch. The roof was covered with clapboards, and the floors were planks, all fashioned from timbers that grew on the farm.

Trees were crosscut into proper lengths for the walls, and slabs were hacked with a double-axe. The sides were hewn flat with a broadaxe. V-shaped notches were cut near the ends so that logs on the sides and ends would mortise-and-tenon into a firm right-angle frame. Other logs were hewn to make the studs, joists and rafters. Some were sawed into short blocks, which were rived with a cleaver to make the clapboards. Still others were ripsawed lengthwise along the grain of the wood to make the planks. At first, the cracks between the logs in the wall were filled with mud; later, mud was replaced with mortar, which was more durable as well as smoother. Everything was done by hand power.

In the cabin were two bedrooms, which were used also as sitting rooms during summertime. They had double beds with feather-bedding and straw mattresses, two or three chairs, a table, a coal-oil lamp, a wood-burning heating stove, a window on the north, and a window and a door on the porch side.

The kitchen on the east end had a window and a door on the north, and a window and a door with a latch string on the porch side. It also contained a large brick fireplace, a wood-burning cookstove, three or four straight-back chairs, a small rocker, a table covered with oilcloth, a coal-oil lamp, and a four-poster bed with wooden pegs cleated to the sides and ends, to which ropes were attached in lattice-work fashion, as a substitute for slats on which to place the straw mattress and feather-bedding.

The fireplace was about five feet wide with depth and height in proportion. Heavy andirons held the wood above the coals, which gave the fire the necessary draft. Large, fire-resistant round backlogs of tough hardwood were placed on the hearth behind the andirons. Some were so heavy and bulky that Tom had difficulty in carrying them from the woodshed and placing them in the fireplace. Fortunately, they burned for two or three days. Small round or split logs were put on the firedogs at the front. Kindling wood or papers or corncobs soaked in coal-oil were placed underneath to start the fire. Soon, a booming fire was going and the sparks began to scintillate across the fireside into the bare-floored room. The fire was attended, so that it rarely went out from the beginning of winter until the coming of spring. It was an effective type of heat.

Grandmother placed supper on the oilcloth table, with the coal-oil lamp in the center. The wick was always neatly trimmed and the globe cleared of smoke, so that the feeble light could be diffused about the room. In fact, the lamp sometimes was dispensed with, as the blaze from the fireplace reflecting from the whitewashed walls lighted the room sufficiently for dining and washing the dishes. Supper often included meat, potatoes, mush, cornbread, molasses, butter, milk, canned fruit and coffee. After Tom had said grace, we all proceeded to enjoy the meal with gusto, for everyone had a healthy appetite.

After the repast, Tom stirred the fire and Grandmother betook herself to her cane rocking chair and picked up her long-stemmed clay pipe. Pinching off a small piece of tobacco from a twist, she chafed it in her hands until the leaves crumbled into small bits. She pressed them gently into the bowl of her pipe, took a small live coal from the embers, and put it on top of the tobacco. Then, leaning back, she enjoyed drawing and puffing on the smoke. Two or three other old ladies within my acquaintance habitually resorted to the weed, a quite normal practice of the day.

During winter the kitchen was used as a sitting room, as it was the only room that could be heated sufficiently when the cold winds raged, forcing their chilling gusts between the mortar and the logs and around the windows and doors.

Sitting in front of the fireplace on a cold winter night when the temperature was below zero was an experience to remember. The torrid heat radiated from the fire against one's face so intensely that one felt uncomfortably hot—while the cold air in the rear of the room circulated against one's back so freely that one felt really cold! Bushes directly outside the house burned in mock imagery of the fireplace blazes.

As we sat around the hearthstone, Grandmother plied me with questions she felt would set my life on the right path.

"What do you study in school?" was one of her favorite questions.

"Everything in my grade, but history is my favorite subject."

"What are you going to do for a living when you grow up?"

"A lawyer, some day, I hope."

"How are you going to be a lawyer, when you don't have any money?"

"I don't know, but there ought to be a way."

"We pay you fifty cents a day, when you work for us. What do you think you will make as a lawyer?"

"Maybe a thousand dollars a year. I don't know, but it ought to be better than being a farmer."

Like all the young, I had more hope than knowledge, but my instincts were leading me in the right direction, though I did not know it at the time.

Tom was more reticent than Grandmother, but he did show real enthusiasm when politics was discussed. He was a diehard Republican and would argue politics at the drop of a hat. His ultra-conservatism later manifested itself when Theodore Roosevelt succeeded to the presidency in 1901, after the assassination of President McKinley. Tom thought the country would go to the dogs, as Teddy was a proclaimed progressive. But Tom was not so narrow that he would not listen to the other side.

The country had gone through the panic of 1893, during the administration of President Grover Cleveland, so the campaign of 1896 was expected to be a lively one. Tom proposed that we go to Mt. Vernon to hear the speeches the next summer, and I accepted with alacrity, for it promised to be a lively time, unlike the daily life on the farm.

As we sat gazing at the fire, the smoke from Grandmother's pipe wafting into the air, floating in a wisp to the fireplace, and being drawn up the chimney with the sparkling blazes into the darkness of the night—the world we knew seemed serene.

About nine o'clock, Grandmother knocked the residue from her pipe, gently tapping it on the brick hearth. Tom banked the ashes over the blazes and flaming coals to smoulder during the night. He retired to the large double bed in the kitchen, while Grandmother and I walked along the long open porch to our separate rooms. A low fire had been set in the bedrooms at night, so going to bed was pleasant.

Before morning, though, the fires had burned out and the rooms were extremely cold. On arising, we hurriedly donned our clothes and hastened along the porch to the kitchen, before we were chilled to the bone. Tom already had shaken the ashes off the logs, removed the accumulation from the hearth, stirred the coals and put new frontsticks on the andirons. The fire was crackling sharply, and so the day began.

Shortly after the sun arose, painting the celestial horizon like a regal tent, Tom and I walked down the lane to the old log barn a couple of hundred yards below the house. There we were to feed the horses and cattle and milk the cows. As we approached, we were welcomed by the horses' neighing and the cows' impatient mooing to be fed. After we finished our chores, we returned to the house. Grandmother had breakfast ready, a solid working man's meal of pancakes or cornmeal cakes, bacon or ham, hominy, molasses, butter, coffee and milk.

One summer the barn became infested with rats. They became so numerous and voracious that they were real pests. They raided the corncrib with such wantonness that it became imperative to find some way to exterminate them. Traps were tried but proved ineffective for such large numbers. Poison was not feasible, as it might kill the horses and cows.

"We have tried everything but shooting them," Tom said desperately.

"Suppose I try a rifle?" I suggested, falling in with his idea.

As the rats ran along the cracks between the logs, I picked them off, one by one, with a .22 caliber rifle. Evidently, they did not like the smell of their own blood, as there was a general exodus and no more rats were to be seen for several months.

Normally, wheat and corn were grown on the ancestral farm, but other crops were also raised. We grew sorghum cane, from which we made molasses. Sorghum seeds were planted in rows like ordinary corn. The plants grew into slender, jointed stalks up to eight feet in height, with long, narrow leaves and a heavy head of seeds. When the stalks were ripe, they were filled with a thick, sweet juice. Harvesting consisted of topping the seeds, stripping the blades, and cutting the cane near the ground.

The juice was extracted by feeding the succulent stalks between a pair of upright iron rollers, rotated by a horse hitched to a sweep and walking around in a circle. The juice pressed from the cane flowed through a sieve into a long box. This strained off some of the extraneous matter. The juice was kept in this box for some time to permit more of the impurities to settle on top. After they were skimmed off, the clarified juice drained into the cooking vat, a long, narrow, shallow pan placed over a wood fire. The juice cooked for a few hours at the near boil. This caused the water to evaporate in a dense steam and the dross to float on top. It sometimes fell to me to scoop off the scum with a skimmer until only the dense, purified liquid remained. The thick, syrupy molasses was preserved in jugs, jars and kegs, and provided one of our few sweeteners, long before the days of granulated sugar.

A ton of sorghum cane produced approximately one-half its weight in juice. The cooking resulted in up to twenty gallons of molasses, whose market price ranged from twenty to thirty cents a gallon.

Another specialty was growing broomcorn, and the manufacture of brooms by hand. Broomcorn seeds were planted in rows by hand and cultivated similarly to sorghum cane. The stalks also were tall and slender, but the tops consisted of elongated, stiff-branched, seed-bearing broomstraws. When the broomcorn was ripe, the stalks were topped with long enough stems to hold the straws and the seeds intact.

After a short period of curing, the seeds were threshed with a homemade, hand-powered seeder, a wooden drum with square, headless nails driven close together on the outside. The contraption was placed in the frame of a wheat fan and rotated with a hand crank attached to a cog wheel. By turning the handle rapidly, the drum was rotated with considerable speed. The seeds were threshed by holding the broomstraws against the nails on the fast rotating drum.

The broom-making machine had a small barrel, a clamp, a spool of broomwire and a foot treadle. The broomhandle was clamped inside the barrel. The loose end of the wire was nailed to its lower end, and the broomstraws were arranged around the handle. The broomstick was rotated by the operator's foot, which wound the wire around the lower ends of the broomstraws. Another nail held the wire and straws in place.

The last step was to sew the straggling straws with twine. This was done by flattening the broom in a press and stitching the straws with a blunt-pointed needle, to keep them from spreading when in use.

My uncle could wire six dozen brooms in one day. It took him about one-half as long to sew them. Then he peddled them about the countryside and in the small villages for twenty-five to thirty cents per broom.

Making apple butter was an annual event which was anticipated with great pleasure by all. It took place outdoors in the fall. Some of the apples were pressed into cider in a hand-cranked cider mill; others were peeled, cored and quartered for making apple butter.

A 20-gallon copper kettle was used for the cooking. Its semi-circular iron ring was suspended over a rigid pole. The kettle was filled almost to the brim with cider. A fire was built underneath, and the juice was boiled down to around one-half its original volume. The cider was removed and the kettle was filled with quartered apples, which were boiled in a small quantity of water until they became a seething mass of apple sauce. The cider was then poured back into the kettle and a small quantity of sugar and cinnamon was added. The mixture was boiled for some time and agitated constantly with a board paddle perforated with large holes. Stirring often fell to me. It required about a bushel of apples to produce two gallons of apple butter. The finished product was stored in large glass and earthenware jars, and it was one of our favorite foods.

Two large cherry trees grew in front of the old log house. During May and June, the branches practically broke under their heavy burdens of ripe red cherries, tantalizingly dangling in the breeze. It was my delight to climb these trees and pick bucketsful of delicious cherries for canning. Also, and to eat my fill in competition with the woodpeckers, bluejays, mockers and catbirds, that darted in and out of the branches snatching their share, even while I was picking.

Apples, peaches and plums were gathered from the orchard, and wild blackberries and raspberries were picked from the briars along the fencerows and the fringes of the woods. These Grandmother canned in glass jars for the larder of the winter season. Hollyhocks and red roses adorned the corners of the yard, adding their beauty to the scene.

It was then the custom for country teachers to room and board on a farm. A teacher of the local Downen School lived with Grandmother and Tom and paid them $10.00 per month. Sometimes he worked on the farm during the vacation in the summer, especially at harvesting and threshing time, helping to earn his keep.

Shortly after the turn of the century, Grandmother and Tom passed on, and the old log house fell into other hands.

Anyone familiar with log houses during the early days, likely would agree with Thoreau that:

"The most interesting dwellings in this country, as the painter knows, are the most unpretending, humble log huts and cottages of the poor."

CHAPTER THREE

Our Country Home

OUR FRAME HOUSE, situated on a long, high hill facing the west, gave us a panoramic view of rolling hills, pleasant valleys, kaleidoscopic patterns of autumn woods, marvelous sunsets and spectacular rainbows. In the summertime we could watch the gathering storms, and in the winter season contemplate with wonder the lustrous ice and glistening snow that turned the visible world into a land of magic.

The four ground-floor rooms were arranged in an L-shape, two in front and two in the rear. Three were bedrooms and the other a combination kitchen-and-dining room. All four were lathed, plastered and papered, and heated with wood-burning stoves. A covered porch was on the western front of the house and an open one within the L facing the north and east.

My bedroom was the large attic space immediately above the two front downstairs rooms. It had a plank floor with wide cracks, and there was no lathing, no ceiling and no stove. The only protection against the weather were the sheathing boards on the sides and gable ends and the shingle roof overhead. In the winter, a large tarpaulin was stretched above the bed across the horizontal beams where the ceiling should have been, to prevent moisture from falling on it.

As a rule, sleeping under the sky, so to speak, was not a real hardship to a stripling youth. The swaying of the trees in unison with the aeolian music in the moonlight, the patter of gentle raindrops on the rooftop during the spring and summer, and the snow muffling much of the noise from the outside world lent enchantment and lulled me into a deep, sound sleep almost as soon as my head came to rest on the pillow. But when the storms came, the mighty winds agitated the nearby forest and the thunder and lightning proclaimed the majesty of the sky.

When blizzards came, the tarpaulin canopy kept the snow, which sifted under the shingles, from falling on the bed. It required considerable fortitude for me to jump from under the warm covers, step barefoot on the thin siftings of granular snow on the uncarpeted floor, don my frosty clothes, and bound down the bare, creaking stairs to the fire in my father's and mother's room below. But children of that era were not coddled, and I expected nothing different.

During cold wintry nights, the water in the buckets in the kitchen became caked with ice and the window panes became translucent with a pellicle of frost from the steam of the singing teakettle. Jack Frost played his nocturnal prank of depicting picturesque ferns, stars and other geometrical designs over this wintry canvas, and it was fascinating to wonder what made frost take these imaginative shapes.

In the beginning our only source of water for domestic use was the rain running off the roof into the cistern inside the L. So much dust settled on the rooftop and washed into the reservoir, though, that it became necessary to empty it and scrub the cement floor and sides once or twice a year. When this procedure was due, as well as in extremely dry weather, we had to haul water in barrels from two springs in the bluegrass pasture several hundred yards down the valley from the house.

These springs were about fifty feet apart, one flowing from one side and the other from the opposite face of the ravine. They had been gushing forth clear, sparkling water in wet as well as in dry weather as far back as any one could remember. The flow commingled in a brooklet, trickled down the rocky rill, glimmering in tiny waves until the level land was reached. Then it flowed gently on to Big Creek a mile away.

The only solution to our water problem was to dig a well. Before deciding upon a location, we engaged a "dowser" or water witch. He had the reputation of being able to find the course of underground water by means of a supple wand. While he was surveying the situation, he attempted to explain his occult and esoteric powers to us.

"Water runs in the ground like it does in a pipe. I will cut a forked limb from this bush and use it as a divining rod. I will hold it in my hands and walk around the yard until the vibrations from my body passing through the wand come into mystical contact with the water. When I pass over the vein, the stem will wiggle and waggle."

"How can the vibrations from your body jump from the end of the forked stem into the ground?" I asked, dubious of such an explanation.

"That is one of the secrets of a dowser, and, if there isn't any water, I won't be able to find it," he said simply.

He cut a Y-shaped supple branch from a hazel bush. The forks were about six inches long and the stem about the same length. He proceeded to explore for water by holding one of the forks in each of his hands and by walking about the yard. We watched him as he carefully went about his divination, which he kept up for about a quarter of an hour. Finally, in an excited and staccato tone of voice, he exclaimed:

"The stick is beginning to move! It is being pulled sideways and downward by the water! It is moving faster and faster! I can hardly hold it! The stem is about to break off! The vein is about fifty feet below! This is where you ought to dig your well!"

The place decided by our water witch was thirty or forty feet from the kitchen door and near the line between the curtilage and the barnyard. The location was very convenient for obtaining water for the house and for the horses and cattle in the barnyard. So we decided to follow the recommendation of our dowser and began to dig our well.

Spades, shovels, picks and dynamite were used in loosening the dirt and the rocks in the wellpit. Hoisting dirt and rocks to the surface was accomplished with a bucket tied to the end of a rope and raised and lowered by means of a crank windlass.

Sometimes the rock strata were so solid that the only way to remove them was to use dynamite. A hole was drilled into the strata with a crowbar. A stick of dynamite with a percussion cap and fuse was inserted into the opening and tamped down with fine particles of rocks. The fuse was lighted with a match. A long fuse was used to give the one in the well time to make his exit before it burned to the detonator. The occupant hurriedly sat astride the bucket and was windlassed hastily to the top.

The explosion came with a noisy blast, cracking the rocks and blowing some of the fragments out of the well. If there was no blast, nobody knew whether the fuse was live or dead. Under these circumstances, reentry into the well was postponed for several hours. Even though there was a detonation, we waited a few hours before resuming the excavation. The hazard of suffocation from the noxious smoke and gas of the dynamite was always present. We were hardy folk—but not foolhardy.

Except for digging through solid rocks, everything progressed smoothly until a depth of about twenty feet was attained. At that level, dampness and underground gas were encountered. A neighbor, who was digging with us, fainted and fell prostrate in the well. My father and I were operating the windlass, and we called in an excited tone of voice:

"John! Are you all right?"

The only response was our own echoes.

We were beset with anxiety, not knowing whether he was alive or dead. I hurriedly bridled and mounted Old Prince bareback and raced him to the home of a neighbor about a half-mile away. Luckily, he was at home and we sped back in the nick of time. He at once descended into the wellpit, detached the bucket from the rope, and tied the rope around the limp body of our disabled victim. We windlassed him to the top of the well and laid him on the grass. The rope was lowered at once, the bucket was reattached, and soon our rescuer was hoisted safely out of the well. The condition of our asphyxiated neighbor was so serious that it was several hours before he was completely resuscitated. After this near tragedy, we waited for two or three days before resuming the digging in order to give the gas time to escape.

At a depth of about forty feet, a good supply of pure, cold water was located. Did this vindicate the water witch and his divining rod, or was it a mere coincidence that water was found? We could never be sure. Some farmers claimed that they, too, had located some fine wells of water with the supple wand even when other methods had failed. Around the turn of the century, one could hear arguments pro and con on this question, and even today, mostly in rural areas, the occasional dowser quietly applies his knowledge—and apparently with significant success.

Water was drawn from our well by attaching an old oaken bucket to each end of a long chain, which ran over a pulley suspended a few feet above the well. As a full bucket was drawn from the well, an empty one was lowered to be filled.

During the winter season, we handsawed ice on the pond and stored the blocks in the ice house under a thick bank of sawdust. The ice lasted well into the summer and was used in, among other things, the country pastime of making ice cream.

Milk and cream with sugar and vanilla were put into a cylindrical metal freezer, which was held upright inside of a wooden cask. Ice and salt were put around the freezer and the contents were frozen by rotating it with a crank at the top of the cask. It took much effort, but that only made it taste all the more delightful.

We slaughtered hogs during the cold weather for home use and for sale in the market. Hog killing was a community affair in which a number of farmers cooperated. The animals were shot with a 22-gauge rifle midway between the ears, and they usually fell with the first bullet, so they felt no pain. The carcasses were doused several times in a barrel of scalding water to soften the bristles, so that they could be scraped off with a sharp butcher's knife. Then they were eviscerated. For the hogs which were to be sold this was the final stage in the process.

Those kept for home use were carved into hams, shoulders and sides. Certain parts were ground into sausage and liverwurst meat in a handmill or grinder. The intestines were flushed, turned inside out, scraped, cleaned and washed, and the ground meat was packed into the casings with a hand-stuffing machine.

As there was no refrigeration, it was necessary to preserve the meat, usually by curing it in the smoke-house. Ordinarily, the smoke-house was constructed of boards and covered with clapboards or shingles. The curing was done by salting the parts down in boxes for a few days, washing off the salt and sprinkling them with pepper, then hanging them over a smouldering fire of hickory or sassafras wood. The salt, pepper and smoke constituted the preservatives, and anyone who has tasted meat so cured will attest to its wonderful flavor.

It was the custom of our father to cut a small tree in the woods and to bring it into the house for the Christmas season. He stood it on the floor and decorated it with patches of cotton to imitate the snow, and with candles to provide the light. On Christmas Eve he would make his entry into the house adorned with cotton whiskers and laden with a bag of presents on his back. These usually consisted of a couple dozen oranges and some stick candy. After lighting the candles, Santa proceeded to divide the gifts among my three sisters and myself. Then he silently slipped out of the room, without another word to us. Not even Aladdin's magic lamp and ring could have lent greater enchantment during our tender years than our father's annual visit as Santa Claus on Christmas Eve.

Around the turn of the century, the only means of communication with the outside world was by foot or horse. During the somber wintertime, when the sun sank below the western horizon and darkness enveloped the landscape, almost all life came to a standstill. Except for the more useful activities of preparing meals and studying our lessons, about the only activity inside our house was playing checkers or "fox-and-geese," with red and white grains of corn for men, on a board which we made ourselves.

The isolation was complete when the snowstorms, ice and sleet storms, and blizzards swooped upon us from the north and west. Usually, Nature gave us sufficient warning to round up the horses, cattle and sheep; to put them in the barn or straw shed; to provide them with a supply of corn, hay and oats; and to carry wood and water into the house for the siege—then there was nothing to do but to wait it out.

During an occasional winter, snow fell for twenty-four to thirty-six hours with little interruption. Sometimes it attained a depth of two or three feet on the level and considerably deeper in the drifts. During a severe blizzard in 1894, the snow was driven at practically hurricane speed, and the temperature fell precipitately below zero. Day practically merged into night. Doors and windows were shaken, rattled and strained by the buffeting winds, as if by angry spirits, and our house felt as if it would be lifted off its foundation. The fires in the heating stoves burned at the double-quick. We put on heavy coats during the daytime and at night placed extra quilts on our beds to keep warm. We could hear the trees swaying and groaning in the tempest, but we could not see them, as the whirling dance of the blinding sheets of snow reduced visibility to a few feet, even during the daytime.

Finally, the storm abated and the sun broke through. Fog retreated from the valleys like white ghosts furtively stalking into the nearby woods. Nothing rough or jagged could be seen. White mounds took the places of rocks and stumps. Small ditches, depressions and roads were smoothed over as evenly as covers on a bed by a woman's hands. Fenceposts appeared as apparitions with snow-white caps. The cheerless pale gray trees drooped disconsolately under their heavy burdens. Our entire world, from horizon to horizon, was enveloped in a dense mantle of white. In the midst of such magnificent sublimity, one could not avoid pondering the absoluteness of the Maker of the Universe and the finiteness of man himself.

But there was little time for meditation. Many chores were awaiting us—the shovelling of paths about the house and the barnyard through deep snow, the feeding and watering of the stock, the milking of the cows, the toting of more wood and water into the house. As we went about our tasks, our breaths floated away in a frozen vapor, and the cold wind caused the blood to race through our veins. Our chests heaved, our voices were husky, and our spines shivered. We rubbed our hands and knuckles briskly and stomped our feet on the ground to keep them from becoming numb.

Many times during cold winter days I have read Whittier's "Snow Bound" nostalgically. He depicted faithfully the isolation and the close family relationship that occurs during a severe snowstorm, which our own family experienced from time to time, especially during that never-to-be-forgotten storm of 1894.

For several days the roads were impassable. Then, as the snow melted and gradually settled, we were able to travel in two-horse sleighs and, still later, in wagons. It took a few weeks before all the snow was gone.

The nights following a blizzard-type snowstorm were clear and cold. The stars sparkled like diamonds in the blue firmament above. Later in the night, the full moon rose like a silver disk and cast uncanny shadows on the ghost-like trees over the snow-covered hills and valleys, making the whole landscape look eerie and desolate.

Less frequent were the icestorms, which occurred during extremely cold weather but which could be just as dangerous. When the raindrops came into contact with roofs, trees, fences, roads and fields, they sometimes froze and formed a solid covering of ice. The weight of the coating was so heavy that some of the tops and branches of the trees cracked under the strain and fell to the ground, shattering the ice into thousands of fragments and causing a resounding crash. It would be difficult to find in Nature a more beautiful spectacle than hundreds of ice-coated trees sparkling in the sunlight or the moonlight and tinkling light jingles in the breeze.

One major icestorm comes to mind. It occurred about 1900 and followed a light snowfall. The crust of the snow was frozen so solid and the ice was so smooth that we were able to skate over the roads and the open fields almost as easily as on the ponds.

After the melting of the snow and the thawing of the earth, smiling spring arrived, bringing out the budding and leafing of the poplars, maples, elms, hickories, sycamores, oaks, walnuts, gums and sassafras, and the flowering of the dogwoods, redbuds, sumacs, and elders. Also, the colorful blooming of the dandelions, violets, morning glories, honeysuckles, roses, mayapples and other early spring flowers lent welcome color and richness to the landscape. There was a mass of coloration of the blackberry, raspberry and gooseberry briars and bushes, and the peach, apple, cherry, pear, plum and apricot trees. In due time, the blooms wilted and every briar, bush and tree became laden with fruit.

Bluebirds and bluejays were decorated with azure on their backs and wings. Cardinals were adorned in scarlet robes. Woodpeckers were decked with yellow bibs. Robins wore aprons of red. Mockingbirds and whippoorwills were wing-marked with white. Blackbirds and crows were painted with coal-tar dye. Catbirds and doves were dressed in slaty gray. Quails and sparrows were camouflaged with streaks of brown and white. The throats of hummingbirds were tinted with ruby red. All built their nests and hatched their young, and each seemed marvelously different.

The bobwhites were the most fascinating. If a person approached too close to the nest, which was on the ground, the mother quail would hop and limp slowly away with a simulated broken wing. She would lead the intruder farther and farther away from her nest until she felt it was safe from molestation. Then she would soar suddenly into the air and leave the interloper wondering how he could have been so easily duped. After her eggs were hatched, she would lead her brood in single file through the sheltered places in the fields along the fencerows and across the roads, clucking and calling to them like a domestic hen, to be sure they followed. When she scented danger, she would give a signal, her chicks would disperse, squat low, and hug the grass and the leaves until she notified them that they were safe.

The redwing blackbirds were not as subtle in protecting their nests as the quails. Instead of employing the partridge's guile, the redwings would make a direct frontal attack at the presumed enemy. The nest usually was located in a small bush, and the male would sit on a post or in a small tree and guard it like a sentinel. If an intruder approached too close to the nest, he would make a dive-bomb sweep at the interloper's head. If this did not drive the intruder away, the bird would sometimes make a swift lateral attack and knock his hat off, or possibly draw blood on his head with a sharp peck.

One spring a pair of robins built their nest in the eaves of our house above the downspout where it joins the wall. We were preparing to paint and asked the painter to skip a space around the nest in order not to upset the birds. Instead, we decided to move the nest with its four sky-blue eggs to a tree a few yards from the house. We had heard the old saying that birds will leave their nests if it has been touched with human hands, so we were much surprised when these robins returned and hatched their young, as though nothing had happened.

Years later I related this experience to an expert on birds. He said he supposed these robins never had heard of this old saw, so they were not bound by it!

The lambs were easier to tame than any other animals on the farm. Sometimes they were weaned on a bottle of cow's milk and later fed from a bucket. One of our pet lambs was as tame as Mary's. We missed her one rainy day and were beset with a foreboding that investigation confirmed. We found her lying on her back, dead in a ditch in the bluegrass pasture.

Teddy, our dog, was named after President Theodore Roosevelt, and he was the most domesticated animal on the farm. At night when we were sleeping, he guarded the house, although there was little need for a sentinel at that time. He did alert us when any unusual noise occurred, such as a fox or weasel invading the chicken house. At milking time he brought the cows in from the pasture. During the hunting season, he chased the rabbits and was a real companion. He fawned upon us for attention and affection, accompanying us up hill and down dale, never faltering. But Teddy contracted the rabies and we had to put him to sleep. Saddened, we gave him a decent burial.

Spring was the time of year when the ducks and geese were robbed of their feathers and the sheep were fleeced of their wool.

It required two persons to perform these operations—one to hold the fowl while the other plucked off its feathers with his fingers, and one to hold the sheep on the shearing table while the other clipped off its wool with a pair of hand shears. During the ritual, the ducks and geese kept up a constant squawking and honking, and the sheep a steady bleating and lamentation. The sheep were put through their ordeal annually, but the ducks and the geese had to endure it only during alternate years. The wool was sold and the feathers were used to make homemade pillows and feather-beds, which were treasured and, if properly made, often lasted a generation or more.

The calendar seemed to turn faster during the spring and summer than at any other time of year. Before we realized it, the summer solstice came and we were "knee-deep in June." During the next two or three months, the sun radiated his scathing heat and light on the farmlands, causing the days and nights to become humid and hot. If the rains came often enough, they tempered the severity of the radiation and nurtured the growing crops. Wheat ripened a golden yellow in time for harvest, the timothy and red clover matured for the haying, the white clover and the blue grass grew luxuriantly for the pasturing, and the corn eared and grew taller, day by day, for the autumn husking—even if raccoons got the occasional ripe ear. That was nature at her best.

Occasionally, however, the caprices of the weather played uncanny tricks on us, as we helplessly watched our labor and even some of our investment vanish in a matter of hours.

Sometimes the days were warm and balmy in the spring, and the trees budded and promised a bountiful yield of fruit. All of a sudden, the weather turned cold and nipped in the bud all hope of any fruit for the year. Now and then, the rains were so scanty that the corn and the clover and the bluegrass on our hill land shrivelled and wilted before our eyes. At other times, the precipitation was so prodigal and so violent that it cut deep gullies in the hillsides and washed the topsoil away. Big Creek overflowed its banks, the floodwaters spread deep over the bottoms, and the corn became flaccid and died, as if Nature had put a curse upon the land.

The devastating effect of the floodwaters was brought home to us in a very striking way. One night as we were sitting on the front porch, a man limped slowly up the road from the direction of Big

Creek, turned into our driveway, then faltered into our yard. As he approached, he fell prostrate on the ground with a sudden thud. He appeared to be exhausted. His hair was tousled, his clothes were rumpled and torn, and he was wet and jaundiced from head to foot.

At that time, country people never locked their doors when they were away from home during the day or at night. Tramps seldom knocked on a farm door for a handout, and robbers and holdup men knew that there were few pickings on the farm. So when the stranger approached us, we felt no more apprehension than we would at a neighbor's walking into the yard.

Walking to where he lay, we asked:

"Friend, who are you and where have you been?"

It was still a few minutes before he managed to rise from his recumbent position and to sit upright on the ground. Then he said:

"My name is Duckworth. I am from the central part of Indiana. I have been peddling veterinary books to farmers in Posey County. I had just finished on the other side of Big Creek and was coming over here to canvass this side."

"What has happened to you?" we asked with concern.

"About four o'clock today, I started to cross Big Creek Bottoms with a horse and buggy. I knew that there had been some heavy rains for a couple of days. When I approached the other side, I could see that the Bottoms were covered with water. I had no doubt, though, that I would be able to make it. I started across, and in a few minutes my horse stepped into a washout and pulled the buggy in with him. He was in water up to the nape of his neck, and the buggy was practically submerged. With considerable difficulty, I was able to extricate myself and to hold onto the top of the buggy. I maneuvered around to the front, unhitched the traces from the whippletree, and loosened the harness from the shaves. Then my horse was able to move out of the deep water and pull me along with him, as I held onto the harness.

"For a time the water was shallow enough for us to proceed slowly. Before long, though, we stepped into deep water again. After struggling and floundering in the muddy water and being bandied about for what seemed to be several minutes, it became necessary for me to abandon my horse and to look after myself. I was terribly confused and baffled, not knowing the exact location of the bridge. My heart began to quail within me, and I bitterly repented my rashness in attempting to go over a strange road covered with swift floodwaters. Somehow or other, I swam when I had to and trod bottom when I could. Finally, I made it to this side of Big Creek, soaked and practically breathless. By that time it was dark. I was so exhausted from the struggle that I had to lie on the ground for an hour or so to rest. Then I pulled myself up the long hill from the Creek, and here I am."

We gave the stranger some dry clothes and put him up for the night. He stayed with us two or three days, until he fully recovered from his ordeal. He told us that he was twenty-two years old and a student at the Indiana University. He said that every spring a representative of a publishing-house appeared at the university to engage students to peddle books during the summer vacation. He chose veterinary books, because he had been brought up on a farm. He usually stayed at a farmer's house overnight and paid about twenty-five cents for his bed and board.

After the floods abated, our sojourner surveyed his damage and discovered that his horse was dead and that there was very little if any salvage value in his buggy.

When it rained and farmers wished that it would stop, or when it was dry and they wished it would rain, very few of them were as philosophical as James Whitcomb Riley:*

WET WEATHER TALK

> They hain't no sense, as I can see,
> Fer mortals, such as us, to be
> A-faultin' Natchur's wise intents,
> And lockin' horns with Providence!
> It hain't no use to grumble and complain
> When God sorts out the weather and sends rain,
> W'y rain's my choice.

---

*From the *Complete Works of James Whitcomb Riley* (New York: Harper & Brothers, 1916), IV:948.

During the resplendent summertime, we sat on our front porch and relaxed under the balmy night, letting nature entertain us. It was our admission-free, open-air amphitheater for marvelling at the sunsets, the thunderstorms, the moon and the stars; and for enjoying the music of the birds, the insects and the frogs. There was nothing to distract our attention from these performances, for not even a horse and buggy passed along the dirt road in front of the house, except on very rare occasions.

Sometimes in summer the elements took on an ominous aspect. The thunder and lightning became so menacing and the downpour so heavy that one might have imagined that Aeolus had untied his bag of winds and Zeus had shot his jagged thunderbolt on Mt. Olympus and loosened all of the rain from the sky, just to fall on us!

At other times, the white, lace-fringed cirrus clouds floated high and majestically above the horizon. Old Sol sent forth his rays and tinted them with pale, pastel colors of blue, yellow and pink. At other times, the cloud-formation was of a massive, mountainous, cumulus type, on which the Artist painted with richer hues of red, purple and gold. These gorgeous spectacles changed tone every moment, as the sun sank gradually below the horizon.

About twilight, the evening concert began, with the vespers of the mockingbird and the robin—the mocker, the most renowned singer of all, trilling its own melodious and tremulous rhapsody and its incomparable imitation of other birds, and the robin intoning its cheery vesper song—as they perched on the topmost branches of the tall sycamore trees in the barnyard.

Shortly after dusk, the insects commenced their chorus, concealing themselves among the leaves of the rosebushes, the maples, the boxwoods and the damson plum trees in the yard. The katydids vibrated their loud syllabic stridulations of "katydid, katydid, katydid," while the cicadas shrieked their shrill, high-pitched tones. Now and then the wind caused a gentle rustling of the leaves, giving the impression that Orpheus was strumming an invisible lyre. When this happened, the chorus was suspended until the zephyr subsided; then the music resumed.

About the time the insect chorus reached its crescendo, we could hear the orchestration of the frogs in the barnyard pond, and in the nearby woods the nocturnal birds—the screech owl screaming its discordant, dismal wailings, and the whippoorwill chanting its plaintive, "whippoorwill, whippoorwill, whippoorwill" as they flew hither and thither in the darkness, seeking prey and acknowledging their whereabouts to their own kind.

In the meantime, the fireflies put on a silent but spectacular exhibition, flitting through the darkness, here, there, everywhere, and intermittently scintillating phosphorescent sparks for a transitory moment, making the darkness seem all the richer in contrast.

To add to the variety, the occasional lowing of the cows, the neighing of the horses, and the baaing of the sheep and their tinkling bells could be heard in the bluegrass pasture in front of the house.

The only visible human habitation was our neighbor's house across the valley. It could be seen by the lamplight gleaming through the windows. Now and then the baying of their dog could be heard floating faintly across the half-mile distance through the stillness of the night.

On dark moonless evenings, we beheld with wonder the North Star, the Big Dipper, the Pleiades and the stars of the Milky Way. On occasion we witnessed with awe the most unusual phenomenon of all, the meteors, as they blazed a temporary path of fire across the sky, seeming to live only for brief seconds.

We observed the moon in all of its cycles, from the thin crescent to the rotund disc. We heard our father say that wet weather was on its way when the crescent stood on its edge and that dry weather was coming when it lay on its back. This was an example of the country folklore in Southwestern Indiana, and millions of farmfolk guided their planting and harvesting by such lore.

About nine o'clock, we abandoned our vigil and went to bed. There would be no roars of automobiles or airplanes to interfere with our slumber during the nighttime or to awaken us prematurely in the early morning hours. But chanticleer would stand tiptoe on his roost at daybreak and sound reveille with his lordly clarion call, a signal to get up and prepare for the day's work.

What an unforgettable experience to arise early in the morning, the most memorable time of day, to feel the gentle, fragrant breeze of morn on one's face, inhale the invigorating ozone, behold for a few moments the rosy fingers of dawn spreading like a giant, open hand in the eastern horizon, see the sun casting his rays over the landscape and dispelling the fogs down in the valley, hear the birds twittering in the orchard, and walk barefoot across the lush pasture through the bluegrass and white clover baptized with pearly drops of dew! No one who has experienced a real country dawn can ever quite forget it.

An unknown Sanskrit author captured the spirit of coming day:*

SALUTATION OF THE DAWN

Listen to the Exhortation of the Dawn,
Look to this Day for it is Life,
   The very Life of Life!
In its brief course lie all of the Verities
   And all the Realities
     Of your Existence:
   The Bliss of Growth,
   The Glory of Action,
   The Splendor of Beauty;
  For Yesterday is but a Dream
  And Tomorrow is only a Vision;
   But Today, well lived,
  Makes every Yesterday a Dream of Happiness
   And every Tomorrow a Vision of Hope.
    Look well, therefore, to this Day!
   Such is the Salutation of the Dawn.

Thoreau said that the early morning wind forever blows the hymn of Creation, but few are the ears that hear it.

Autumn brought the sense of the end of all this ease and beauty, yet it was the season of ripe, luscious apples, pears and peaches in the teeming orchards, sparkling cider in the barrels, apple butter,

---

*From *Masterpieces of Religious Verse,* ed. James Dalton Morrison (New York: Harper Brothers, 1948), p. 301. The poem is by an unknown Sanskrit poet, circa 1200 B.C.

jams, jellies and fruits in the jars, golden fodder in the shocks, hoarfrost on the pumpkins, and red, white and yellow ears of corn ready for the shucking pegs. It was the time of gorgeous coloration of the leaves with their gradual change in hues—yellow elms and poplars, russet oaks, tawny gold maples, crimson gums and sumacs, and garnet creepers, lending enchantment to brilliant fall days in a last exciting burst of glory.

Gradually the colorful foliage withered on the stems, and finally, except for stragglers, they were snatched away by the autumn gusts and blown helter-skelter from place to place, until eventually the rains and snows weighted them down for their long sleep—creating a mood of sadness and loss in the last autumn days.

When the migratory birds winged their way over the skyways on their southern flight, we realized that winter was coming, and that the cycle of the seasons would begin all over again.

Around the turn of the century, country houses had no running water. Water had to be drawn from the cistern or well and carried in buckets into the house. Zinc washtubs were used for taking baths in the kitchen or smokehouse. Vice President Marshall, who hailed from Indiana, used to say that Hoosiers took baths only on Christmas and the Fourth of July. The only toilet facility was the little frame two-seated outhouse fifty or so yards back of the house.

A glass kerosene lamp was used for illumination. About 1900, a metal gasoline lamp became available on the market. Gasoline instead of kerosene was placed in the bowl and a pump was used to transmute it into gas. Instead of a wick, it had a lacy mantle. Ignited with a match, it radiated a white, luminous, incandescent light throughout the room, a great improvement in visibility.

Around the turn of the century, a number of events took place which mitigated the hardships of country life.

The telephone came as a godsend to country folks. The box was fastened to the wall and the phone was rung by turning a crank. Each party had a special ring—longs and shorts—similar to transmitting a telegram. For the first time, country folks were able to call the doctor without making a trip by foot or horseback, possibly in the middle of the night. When the line was new, someone usually was eavesdropping to learn what was going on or gossiping with the neighbors.

About 1902, rural free-delivery mail-service was inaugurated in Posey County. Depending upon the condition of the dirt roads, the mail carrier made his rounds by horseback, cart or buggy. When Big Creek flooded the roads, it sometimes was hazardous for him to go through the bottoms. A former rural carrier from another section of the country told me that when the roads of his route were inundated, he sometimes took off his pants and rode through the floodwaters on horseback, holding aloft his mailbag and his pantaloons.

The early carrier was paid around $50.00 per month. For this sum he furnished one horse, sometimes two, and cart and buggy to make the trip daily including Saturday. He was known personally by all of the people on his route and acted as a conveyor of country news and gossip, as well as a carrier of the mail, so his arrival was anticipated as an important and welcome event.

Prior to rural free delivery, as it was officially named, we had to go to Oliver Station three or four miles away to pick up the mail. This usually was done on Saturday night in order not to interfere with the farm work.

It was the automobile, however, which brought about the most revolutionary change in country life. It made its advent shortly after the turn of the century with the introduction of the Ford Model T. Depending on the condition of the roads, it had a speed of fifteen to twenty-five miles. It could not be used during a part of the winter season or even in summer during rainy weather, due to the condition of the unimproved roads. Its very existence forever separated the past from the present, which thereafter was to become increasingly mechanized.

Farmers were called upon to spend two or three days in the spring with a team of horses or mules grading, dragging, ditching and otherwise keeping the roads in a state of repair, or to pay a road-tax in lieu of such work, as the auto became king.

The wagon, however, continued to be used for heavy loads, and two horses or mules were required to pull it. It took about a full day to haul a load of wheat, corn, hogs or cattle to market in Evansville, fifteen miles distant and to return home with an empty load. The road to Parkers Settlement was dirt-surfaced; from there on to town, it was covered with loose gravel. Now and then we left a couple of sacks of wheat or corn to be ground into flour or meal at a grist mill on Bunker Hill on the hither side of Evansville, and we picked up the grist on the way home.

At that time, farmers could buy a glass of beer for a nickel, and have a free lunch of cheese, bologna, liverwurst and crackers, when they had the time for it. They were expected to buy more than one glass, and they usually did, for they did not often have much free time; when they did, they greatly enjoyed the occasion.

A hired hand's wages ranged from ten to fifteen dollars a month, lodging and board included. During wheat-harvesting, the wage rose to two dollars and at corn-shucking, one dollar a day. Very little work was done on the farm during the wintertime, except clearing the land, so it was not uncommon for a hand to work solely for his keep during the winter season, and to be glad to have a place to stay.

Most of our food was grown on the farm: fruit, vegetables, milk, butter, eggs, chicken, lard, pork and beef. Our wheat was ground into flour and our corn into meal, as needed. So the relative lack of money in those days must be considered in the light of that fact.

The approximate prices we paid for articles bought in the stores were: coffee, twenty cents a pound; sugar, four cents; salt, three cents; crackers, five cents; tea, twenty-five cents; candy, ten cents; canned vegetables, eight cents; canned fruit, twelve cents a can; vinegar, thirteen cents; and molasses, twenty-five cents a gallon.

In half-dozen lots—and sterling silver, at that—teaspoons cost three dollars and fifty cents, tablespoons eight dollars and fifty cents, knives and forks eight dollars and fifty cents. Ordinary ware, which was used on the farms, cost much less.

A kitchen or heating wood-burning stove cost seven dollars and fifty cents; a sewing machine, twenty dollars. Women's suits were about four dollars and fifty cents; shoes, two dollars; cotton stockings, five cents; and hats, two dollars. Men's suits ranged from four to six dollars; shoes, one dollar and seventy-five cents; socks, twelve cents; overcoats, ten dollars.

A watch could be bought for a dollar, and a gold-plated one for two dollars and seventy-five cents; and many made in those days are still in good working order.

An axe cost sixty-five cents; a hatchet, thirty-eight cents; a handsaw, one dollar; a hammer, twenty-five cents; a plow, four dollars and fifty cents; a sulky riding plow, twenty-four dollars and seventy-five cents; a disc-harrow, sixteen dollars and seventy-five cents; a top buggy, thirty dollars; and a surrey with tassels on the top, forty-five dollars.

A hotel room in Mt. Vernon rented at about a dollar and a dinner cost twenty-five cents, but what farmer would have paid a dollar for a room around the turn of the century! He would have been thought extravagant in the extreme.*

---

*Table 122 of the Consumer Price Index of the Handbook of Labor Department Statistics, 1975 Reference Edition, Bulletin 1865, gives the following comparison of the purchasing power of the dollar in 1913 and 1974, assuming the purchasing power of the dollar for

$$1967 = \$1.00$$
$$1913 = \$3.367$$
$$1974 = \$ .687$$

The 1967 dollar's purchase power was equal to 29.7 cents of the 1913 dollar, and the 1974 dollar was equal to 20.1 cents of the 1913 dollar in purchasing power. The Federal Reserve Board indicated the March 1978 dollar's purchasing power was equal to 15.7 cents of the 1913 dollar.

To compare the 1900 prices shown above with the present-day dollar, it would be necessary to multiply them by seven or eight or probably more.

CHAPTER FOUR

Clearing the Land

THE MOST BEAUTIFUL parts of the country in Southwestern Indiana were the woods, with their verdant foliage during the spring and summer, their variegated coloration in the autumn, and their solemn majesty during the winter season. In the summertime, the trees tended to lose their individuality in a mass of foliage, except the spreading oaks and stately poplars, which towered over the others like Goliath over David. After the leaves fell, each tree regained its identity. The oaks and poplars still took the prize for magnificent stature. The reward went to the beech for the beauty of its bole, the symmetry of its bare limbs, divided and subdivided into the smallest twigs, and for the picturesqueness of its outline against the sky.

About one-half of our farm was covered with virgin forest. As the arable acreage was too small for economical farming, our father decided to clear a portion of the woodland, which was a formidable task in a day before power-saws and bull-dozers.

Before we began our devastation, it was my privilege to walk over the leafy carpet in the woods and marvel at the handiwork of Nature in creating such magnificent trees. Some of the oaks and poplars were four feet or more in diameter and in excess of 75 feet in height. A sylvan temple with venerable columns crowned with verdant capitals!

It was an unforgettable experience to stand beneath the rustling foliage in the early morning, as the sun gradually penetrated the shadows and cast flickering sunbeams through the sylvan canopy onto the ground. The twittering of the birds in the bushes and the swaying of the trees in the morning breeze were as musical as the lyre. The squirrels, objecting to any intrusion into their domain, chattered incessantly upon getting a glimpse of me or hearing the slightest tramp of my feet over the dry leaves. They scampered up the trunks of the trees to hide among the leafy branches and to scold me for my intrusion. Sometimes they gave themselves away by letting their tails hang over the limbs. The cardinals in their scarlet robes darted in and out of the bushes like flaming torches ready to set the leaves on fire. The jays, too, added a merry note as they flitted here and there with a piece of the sky on their backs and wings, their piercing call immediately identifiable, no matter how many other bird calls could be heard.

A visit to the woods during a drizzling rain was an experience long to be remembered. Crystal globes dropped from the foliage as I walked over the soaked leaves. Myriads of mayapples shimmered and sparkled with small spheres on their tiny parasols. Cobwebs twinkled with thousands of diminutive beads enmeshed in their gossamer threads. The drenched parasitic mosses on the north sides of the trees radiated verdant beauty. Standing motionless for a spell, watching the birds perched on the nearby bushes, hearing the squirrels jumping from branch to branch, and the raindrops falling from the leaves of the trees, gave me a sensation of peaceful rapture, I still clearly recall.

Another personal pilgrimage I well remember was made at twilight, when the shadows were beginning to envelop the sea of foliage. The trilled chorus of the insects, the plaintive chanting of the whippoorwills, the doleful hooting of the owls, the vesper lays of the mockingbirds and the robins, and the chirping of the other birds serenaded the oncoming night. Gradually, every sound subsided and Silenus began to hold court.

Why, I have since wondered, should one ignore the sanctuaries of Nature and adore only the temples and monuments raised by frail hands? I am happy to see, today, so many young people returning to the instinctive love of Nature which, for so many years seemed threatened to be crushed under the Juggernaut of civilization.

But aestheticism had to give way to the realities of existence. For the sake of cultivation, we destroyed this ancient cathedral, which had taken Nature centuries to build. It was a common tragedy in fulfilling the destiny of the nation in the western march to the Rockies and beyond.

We felled the saplings and small bushes with an axe, the indispensable tool of the pioneers. The air was filled with muffled and rhythmic beats and reverberating echoes from the neighboring hills and valleys, as we chopped them down and split them into wood for the heating and cooking stoves. The medium-sized walnuts, catalpas, locusts and mulberries were sawed into posts and split into rails for the worm fences, due to their imperviousness to decay. The large oaks, poplars, ash, black walnuts and gums were felled with a saw and crosscut into sawlogs for lumber. Trees that were unfit for either fenceposts or lumber or were not needed for firewood were sawed for rolling. The undergrowth and the branches of the felled trees were piled in heaps and burned, after drying for a season.

Felling a tree was started by chopping a notch above the sawline on the fall side. Then, two of us drew the deeply-notched saw blade back and forth on the opposite side, as in a tug-of-war. This cut the bark and sapwood and severed the wood to the center of the trunk. Beyond that point, the transection was the reverse—from the inner rings, beginning with the birth of the tree, to the outer rings near its time of death. The tangy smell of sawdust was richly fragrant.

After the saw became embedded in the trunk, the weight of a heavy tree pinched it and made it difficult for us to pull the saw back and forth. To ease the pressure, we drove an iron wedge into the kerf with a wooden maul. This lifted the burden sufficiently to ease the drag and tilted the tree slightly in the direction of the fall. As the saw reached the far side, we withdrew a safe distance. Soon, the tree fell with a resounding crash, swaying and downing the bushes and small trees standing in its way. Thus a tree died, leaving only a stump for a monument—and only a temporary one at that,

36

as stumps rotted in a few seasons and were pulled out.

Sometimes a surprise was in store for us when we felled a large tree. On one occasion, a coon was evicted from his den in the hollow of the tree when it crashed onto the ground. Our dog, Teddy, took it on for a fight, but the coon was too agile and vicious for his adversary. Before long, it was able to escape by climbing another tree. Another time a colony of wild bees was ousted from its hive in the cavity of the tree, when it bounced onto the ground. The bees put on a display of flying around and buzzing in protest against their eviction, and we kept to a safe distance. On occasion, squirrels, too, had to make a fast move to save themselves when the tree fell. Usually, due to their agility, they were able to jump onto another tree before the felled tree reached the ground.

Delivering doughty blows with an axe or a maul was not a romantic pastime. It required a tower of strength to sink an axe deeply into a hardwood tree and to drive a wedge into the slit of a standing tree with a heavy maul. Even this was less grueling than felling a standing tree or sawing it into logs as it lay prone on the ground. On felling it, we had to bend over at right angles in order not to cut the stump too high above the ground. On crosscutting it, it was necessary to stoop lower and lower as the saw made its way through the trunk to the ground.

A sawmill was brought to our farm to saw the best logs into lumber. It consisted of a steam traction engine, a large circular saw, a track and carriage, and a turning device. The scattered logs were encircled with a chain and rolled onto log wagons over skids with a team of horses, then hauled to the mill. There they were clamped onto the carriage, which moved them head-on against the fast-rotating saw. With the turning device, the operator shifted them into different positions. The saw ripped off the slabs and ripsawed the squared timbers into boards, two by fours, joists and beams, as best suited their conformation. Other members of the crew toted the slabs and lumber away from the mill and stacked them into piles, and shovelled the sawdust out of the pit.

Rolling the logs unfit for posts or lumber or not needed for firewood, was another of those community affairs in which neighborhood farmers helped one another. Two or three smooth handspikes of seasoned hickory or oak wood were laid on the ground and the logs were rolled onto them. The men bent over, took hold of the ends of the spikes, and slowly lifted the heavy burdens until they could stand upright. Then they rolled the logs off the spikes onto piles. After drying for a few weeks, the logs were burned. Only stumps and ashes remained as reminders of once-living trees.

A few years after the land was cleared, the stumps had decayed sufficiently so they could be dug out of the ground and thus an obstacle to cultivation was removed. The dirt was shovelled from the roots, which were then chopped off. Next, the stumps were pried out of the ground by using a fencerail or a pole as a lever, and a rock or piece of wood as a fulcrum. The force was exerted by throwing the weight of our bodies on the upper part of the lever.

Some of the stumps had such large taproots that it was impossible to sever them by the use of the axe. In those cases, we bored a hole in the taproot and inserted a stick of dynamite and a fuse. We ignited the fuse with a match and hotfooted it away to a safe distance. It was not safe to return to a stump immediately after an explosion, due to the noxious smoke and gasses. By returning too soon, one might become dizzy and blinded and have to take to bed and be under a doctor's care. That was an experience of my own during my early days on the farm, when I did not allow enough time for fumes to dissipate.

Occasionally, during the clearing of our land, we found tools of the aborigines, such as a hafted, smoothed stone tomahawk or a flaked flint arrowhead. These the Indians used prior to surrendering their lands to the United States at the beginning of the nineteenth century.

Both the tomahawk and the arrow were instruments of peace as well as weapons of war. The old saying, "They buried the hatchet," is reputed to have originated with the custom of the redmen of giving the tomahawk a ceremonial burial at the end of intertribal hostilities.

CHAPTER FIVE

Planting and Cultivating

GOOD HUSBANDRY of the land called for the rotation of crops, and one of them was clover. It was the first to be sowed during the year. We usually sowed the seed on land that had produced wheat or corn for two or three seasons and thus used up some of its chemicals. Clover seeds were sometimes dispersed over frozen ground. In this way, the seeds became embedded in the soft earth as the ground thawed.

Clover seeds were scattered by means of a portable, mechanical broadcaster, a canvas bag with a round wooden bottom to hold the seed, a strap to go around the sower's neck, a fan fastened to a pivot attached to the wooden bottom, and a rod in the nature of a fiddler's bow. As the sower moved over the ground "fiddling," the seeds trickled out of the bag against the fast-rotating fan. The blades scattered them over quite a swath at each side and in front, giving fairly uniform dispersal.

Clover restored nitrogen to the soil and made good hay for the livestock. It also furnished nectar to the bees in their fabulous process of honey making. Its flowers were as fragrant as orchard blossoms and the bloom of the spring flowers—a sure sign of spring.

James Whitcomb Riley expressed his love of clover in his poem:

THE CLOVER

And so I like clover—it seems like a part
Of the sacredest sorrows and joys of the hart;
And wherever it blossoms, oh, thare let me bow

And thank the good God as I'm thankin' Him now;
And I pray to Him still fer the stren'th when I die,
To go out in the clover and tell it good-bye,
And lovin'ly nestle my face in its bloom
While my soul slips away on a breth of perfume.*

Corn planting took place in the spring. In newly cleared land, the soil was turned over with a John Deere steel walking–plow. The reins encircled our waist, so we could guide the team without the use of our hands, which were engaged in holding the plow in the furrow. We also steered the team with our snappy commands of "giddap," "gee," "haw" and "whoa!"

The John Deere had a perpendicular cutter blade extending from the beam to the point of the plowshare. It cut the sod and the rootlets and prevented the share from becoming stuck under the roots of the stumps. It sometimes cut into a root so deeply that the team was brought to a dead halt. Occasionally, the plow jumped over a root and out of the ground with a sudden jerk, yanking the man behind the plow headlong the length of the beam. He then retracted the reins and dragged the plow back into position in the furrow. Now and then, a copperhead snake was turned out of the ground, which called for considerable agility on one's part to avoid being struck by the deadly creature. As one plodded his weary way homeward at the end of a day, he felt he had earned a good night's rest. He could not forget, though, that tomorrow would be another day just like today, so plowing time was not much looked forward to.

The next step was harrowing, dragging and rolling of the soil, after which came the planting of the corn. A drill was used to drop the seeds, one by one, in a single row. After the plants grew a couple of inches high, they were cultivated with a double-shovel plow. It split the middle between the rows and moved the loose dirt around the tender stalks. This plow was pulled by a horse or mule, first on one side and then on the other side of the row. The corn

---

*From the *Complete Works of James Whitcomb Riley* (New York: Harper & Brothers, 1916), III:854.

was laid by with the second or third tilling, depending upon the state of the grass and weeds.

While walking behind a double-shovel plow on a hot summer's day, one might calculate that if the rows were laid end to end and doubled, the distance covered from early morning to late afternoon would be six or seven miles. And not on solid ground but on soft earth that took strength from a man's legs.

Usually, the sprouts and weeds grew so luxuriantly on newly cleared land that it became necessary to cut them at least twice during the summer. This chore usually fell to the junior members of the family. Chopping sprouts and weeds in a cornfield on a hot summer day with a hoe was tedious and unpleasant exercise. Mourning doves sometimes sat on an elm tree at the edge of the field, emitting their plaintive cries. We called them raincrows, as we believed them to be harbingers of rain. Their mournful notes floating over the heat waves, which we called "lazy lawrence," were welcome music to our ears. We tried to convince ourselves that rain would come and give us a respite from our monotonous toil. But we were often not that lucky.

Worse than the weeds were the chinch bugs, which sapped the tender stalks, and the grub worms, which cut them underground. This was before the general use of chemical insecticides, and very little could be done to counterattack these parasites.

Oats was a spring crop, which was sowed, harvested and threshed in the same manner as wheat.

Wheat was a fall crop. The bald type was easier to harvest and thresh, due to its comparatively smooth, small beards. The bearded kind grew long, awned beards, which were annoying at harvesting and threshing due to their cutting and scratching tendencies.

The land was turned over with a cast-iron walking or riding plow drawn by two or three mules. Then it was harrowed, dragged, disced or rolled, depending upon the condition of the soil. A two-wheeled, horse-drawn wheat drill, with hollow, blunted hoes extending from the seed box to the ground, was used for sowing wheat. As the team pulled the drill forward, the seed trickled through small holes in the seed box and fell into the narrow furrows made by the hoes. It was covered with the loose soil falling back into the grooves. All the time, one of us guided the team while walking behind.

The hoe has been in use for thousands of years in the planting and cultivation of crops. At first, a crooked stick, a ram's horn, or a sharp rock served as a primitive hoe. It was a slow, back-breaking, ineffectual method of planting and cultivating the scanty grain for a meager subsistence. Edwin Markham in his poem, "The Man With The Hoe," portrayed the plight of the farmer back through the corridors of time:

> Bowed by the weight of centuries he leans
> Upon his hoe and gazes on the ground,
> The emptiness of ages in his face,
> And on his back the burden of the world.

Millet, in his famous painting, "The Man With The Hoe," on which the Markham poem was based, pictures even more vividly the servitude of man with a hoe.

The American Indians used the hoe to plant and to cultivate their corn. This method was still in use by our forefathers for planting until the 1830s.

The earliest known plow was a forked limb of a tree, used to scratch the soil superficially for a skimpy seedbed. Drawings in Egypt and Mesopotamia as early as 6,000 B.C. show a forked contrivance, with the longer fork representing the beam and the shorter one the plow. The power to pull it was furnished by a slave.

Amazingly, no significant change was made in this crude method of plowing until the turn of the nineteenth century, except for the substitution of animal for human power. Drawings in Babylonia about 4,000 B.C. depict animals hitched to chariots.

Oxen were used for thousands of years as beasts of burden. Until about 1830, they were the chief source of animal power even in the United States. They were not entirely superseded by horses and mules until about the middle of the nineteenth century. At first, the yoke was applied to the horns of the oxen and later to their necks.

The horse collar was invented about 1,000 A.D. It was fastened around the neck of the horse or mule, and the shoulders became the focal point for pulling the load.

The wooden plow, with some improvements, such as patches of steel fastened over the moldboard, was in use in this country as late as 1837 or later. Due to its cumbersomeness, it required two men to operate it, one to hold it in place in the furrow and one to drive the oxen to pull it—sometimes as many as six. Even with this animal power, a wooden plow was capable of turning over less than an acre a day. The cast-iron plow and the plow with interchangeable parts invented in 1797 and 1814 were not practical on newly cleared land on account of their brittleness, or in gumbo soil, due to their failure to scour. These difficulties were overcome with the invention of the steel moldboard plow in 1837. The next important improvement was the sulky riding plow, which made its advent in 1864. For the first time the farmer was able to ride. A few minor improvements were made between the 1860s and the turn of the century.

The harrow probably was of as great antiquity as the plow. It was mentioned in the Bible and by the pagan writers of Rome. Originally, it was a forked limb of a tree with the small branches cut off, leaving stubs for teeth. A log was tied on top to hold the harrow down, and oxen were used to pull it over newly scratched surfaces. Later, it was developed into a V-shaped wooden frame with wooden pegs inserted for teeth. In time, iron teeth were substituted.

Broadcasting by hand was the method used in sowing seed as far back as history records. The fellaheen scattered the seed over the alluvium along the River Nile after the recession of the annual floodwaters and drove swine over the ground to trample it in. On dry land, it was the custom to broadcast by hand and to drag branches of trees or crude harrows over the soil to cover the seed.

The first patent on a seeding machine in this country was issued in 1799. This drill did not meet with general approval. About 1841, a device was invented which delivered and regulated the volume of seed in the ground. It was claimed that this drill made two bushels of seed go as far as three broadcast by hand, and that it increased the yield from six to eight bushels per acre. Despite these improvements, broadcasting by hand continued to be used in this country to some extent until the 1870s.

Inasmuch as corn is a native product, the corn planter was strictly an American invention. The wheelbarrow-type of drill made its advent in 1828. It could plant six to ten acres of corn in a day, compared to one-half acre by hand with a hoe. Improvements continued to be made until 1890, when the single-drop corn planter was introduced. This was the type we used around the turn of the century.

The plow with a single shovel was placed on the market around 1820, and about 1850 a second shovel was added. By 1870, a two-horse riding cultivator capable of plowing both sides of a row of corn at the same time was invented. Due to the roots and stumps, it was not practical on newly cleared land. It was a decided advantage on old land, however, as it reduced the time for cultivation by at least one-half.

CHAPTER SIX

Harvesting and Threshing

IN JUNE THE WHEAT was ripe for harvesting. A McCormick reaper drawn by three horses or mules was used to cut the grain. A reel rotating clockwise at the front tilted the standing grain against the fast-moving cutting knife. The severed straws fell onto a canvas platform, which carried them to an elevator. It lifted them to a knotter, which tied them in bundles with binder twine; then a kicker knocked them onto a carrier. When it became loaded, the driver released the carrier with the pressure of his foot, and the bundles fell to the ground in rows for shocking.

Two of us did the shocking. We stood the bundles on their butt ends with their heads inclined inward so as not to fall apart. When several bundles were assembled, we broke the straws of two or three of them to make caps to place over the shocks to protect them against the rain.

Although shocking wheat on a hot summer day was an onerous chore, sometimes a little fun broke the monotony. A wheat field was an ideal place for young rabbits to frolic at harvesting time. As the standing grain was reduced, the noise of the binder scared them into the open. Our dog, Teddy, ran helter-skelter after them as they attempted to escape through the golden stubble. When one of them ran towards us, we joined in the chase by sprinting and plunging headlong to the ground in an effort to grab it. Usually it was a narrow miss, but now and then we were lucky to have one for supper.

Grain in the corners of the field could not be cut by the binder, so a cradle was used for this purpose. It was similar to a scythe, except that it had four wooden fingers arranged parallel to the blade. They were used to hold the severed straws with the heads all in one direction and to drop them to the ground in bunches for easy binding. They were bound in bundles with several straws as a binder.

Wheat-threshing was the most spectacular event on the farm. It usually took place shortly after the Fourth of July. Several farmers formed a threshing ring to help. The thresher was moved from farm to farm by a steam, coal-burning, traction engine. The engine and the separator or thresher were usually placed near the barn about seventy-five to one hundred feet apart. The power was transmitted to the separator by means of a wide endless belt, which encompassed the flywheel on the engine and a smaller pulley on the cylinder of the separator. The belt crossed itself about midway between the engine and the separator, for two reasons. One, to keep it from flying off the flywheel; the other, to rotate the cylinder counterclockwise, so as to draw the wheat straws into the separator.

The bundles of wheat were carried from the fields in heavy loads. One wagon was driven on each side of the separator. The bundles were pitched onto a platform, and a man on each side cut the binding twine. A third man standing between them fed the straws into the fast rotating cylinder.

The engine chugged, puffed, flapped and lashed its belt rhythmically, emitting a dense cloud of smoke, as the steam laboriously turned the flywheel over and over.

The grain and the chaff were threshed from the straws by the fast rotation of the cylinder. The chaff was winnowed from the grain by fast vibrating sieves and high-powered fans. The wheat was then funneled through a spout to the side of the separator, sacked and hauled to the granary. The straws and the chaff were blown through the windstack onto the strawpile, which sometimes covered a framework of timbers to make a warm inside shelter for the stock in wintertime. During the threshing, the three men

46

standing on the deck of the thresher were enveloped in a whirlwind of dust so thick that one wondered how they were able to breathe, for once started, threshing was a virtually non-stop operation.

One of the duties of country boys was to carry jugs of water to the men at threshing time. The custom was to carry a jug of whiskey, also, which our neighbor German farmers called "Schnapps." Some of the men were so hot that they were dripping with sweat. Despite this, no one to my knowledge ever refused to take a good swig of whiskey or to wash it down with a chaser of water.

My uncle, Rev. Arthur C. Blackburn, a resident of Posey County, captured the threshing scene in his poem:

THE WHEAT THRESHING

Early morn by rising sun
The thresher whistle blew.
The engineer was always first
To call the threshing crew.

Wagons began to rumble in
From all surrounding farms,
With men and boys to thresh the wheat
Down at the old farm barns.

Housewives also came along
To help prepare the meals
And daughters too who cheerfully
Joined in the work with zeal.

The water boy with horse and cart
Was always present here.
With jug and water for the hands,
He always brought good cheer.

The old steam power and wooden thresher
Was a nineteenth century thing,
It threshed the bundles, stacked the straw,
And screened and fanned the grain.

Each one had his part of work,
None shirked throughout the day,
Some hauled the bundles from the field,
Some hauled the grain away.

A respite came with each noon hour,
First were the horses fed,

All gathered in the dining hall
Of the old pioneer homestead.

And here 'twas said with table spread,
These folks lived off the land,
A better meal was never served
Since the days of Abraham.

And in that day of forks and hoes,
Two-horse plow and reaper;
The spirit of the folklore was,
I am my brother's keeper.*

Haymaking also came during the hot summer months. Timothy or clover was cut with a two-horse mower. If the weather was cloudy or rainy, it was necessary to ted the hay so it would dry. This consisted of scattering any bunches and lifting the hay so the sun could accelerate the curing. After it was properly cured, it was hauled to the barn and pitched into the hayloft through a gable door or window.

The laboriousness of this method was alleviated around the turn of the century by an invention which eliminated the pitching of the hay by hand.

Sometimes clover was permitted to ripen and to be cut for seed. It was then threshed in a machine similar to a wheat separator.

In late August or September, before the blades wilted, the corn was ready to cut for fodder. We tied at least four stalks from two adjacent rows together with a piece of binder twine to form a frame. Holding a machete-type knife in one hand, we bent the standing stalks into the arched elbow of the other arm and cut them with a single stroke of the blade. When we had an armload, we flung the blade into the ground and stacked the cut stalks against the shock. This was kept up until the field was dotted with sheaves of golden Indian corn. Fodder supplemented the other feed for the stock, such as corn, hay and oats.

Corn-shucking arrived in the late November or in December, after the stalks were dry. The ears were husked with a hand shucking peg. It was a piece of slim, bent steel, blunt-pointed at the

*Printed with the author's permission.

upper end and riveted to a leathern mitt, fitted to the palm and buckled with a strap around the back of the hand. The pointed end of the peg was inserted under a narrow strip of husk at the tassel end, which was pulled down to the butt end of the ear. The rest of the shuck then was stripped down and the entire covering was nipped off at the base of the cob. As the ears were husked, they were tossed into the wagon and later stored in the corn crib. The best shucker could husk about seventy bushels of corn in a day with a hand shucking peg, though champions at county fairs were known to more than double that amount.

The first known implement used in cutting grain was the prehistoric, straight-handled, curve-bladed sickle. It was first made of crude stone; later, of copper or bronze; and finally, of steel. By bending low, grasping a few straws in one hand and cutting them with a steel sickle held in the other, a farmer could cut a half-acre of grain in a day. A few years ago, I saw farmers in India and Turkey harvesting wheat in this very manner. The little donkeys, which were used to carry the grain out of the fields, were laden with so many bundles that one could hardly see their heads and legs. I wondered at the backwardness of this primitive method in a day of so much mechanical improvement.

At some later, unknown date, the sickle was improved into a scythe, which had a longer curved blade and a longer handle with two holds for the operator's hands. During the nineteenth century, the scythe was further improved into a cradle by adding four wooden fingers parallel with the blade, which were capable of holding the straws so they could be bunched for easy binding. The scythe and the cradle were imported from Europe around 1800. A farmer could cut several times as much grain with a scythe or cradle as with a sickle.

A horse-drawn reaper was invented by McCormick in 1831, making it possible for the first time to cut grain with horsepower. It could harvest several times as much grain as a man with a scythe or cradle, and many times as much as a man with a sickle. The horse-drawn reaper lifted the burden of cutting grain by hand from the backs of men. It shortened the harvest season and rendered less likely the loss of the crop due to rainy weather. Even with this reaper, the sheaves had to be bound by hand with some of the cuttings, similarly to the grain cut with a scythe or a cradle. About 1878, a knotter was invented which automatically tied the bundles with binder twine and did away with all human power in the harvesting of wheat, barley and oats, with the exception of shocking the bundles. At last the farmer was truly relieved of much of his back-breaking labor.

From the beginning of recorded time until about the middle of the nineteenth century, the method of threshing was by beating the wheatheads with flails, or by walking animals over the straws on the threshing floor to trample out the grain. It was still necessary to winnow it from the chaff by shaking it through small hand sieves. By this method, it was possible to thresh only a few bushels of wheat during an entire day. This crude method is still practiced in some European and in most of the Asiatic countries, as I personally observed on a number of occasions.

In 1845, a mechanical thresher was invented which could thresh twenty to twenty-five bushels of wheat in one hour, with a four-man crew and six to eight horses to furnish the sweep power. This thresher was improved further, and by 1850 the steam engine replaced animal power.

Corn is a native American product; consequently, husking had no history prior to the coming of the English to this country, other than among the Indians. Even beyond 1900, the hand shucking peg was still in use for husking corn.

Incredible as it may seem, the farmers in this country were using practically the same methods of harvesting and threshing grain as the ancients, until the late 1920s. Then, almost overnight more improvements were made in farming implements than had been made from the dawn of history up to that time. The Report of the Secretary of Agriculture during the late 1920s contained the following statement regarding these phenomenal changes:

> Could a farmer of Pharaoh's time have been suddenly rein-carnated and set down in our grandfather's wheat fields, he could

have picked up the grain cradle and gone to work with a familiar tool at a familiar job. And then within the space of twenty years, the methods of production underwent greater changes than they had in the previous 5,000 years. At one stride, we covered more ground where fifty centuries had left almost no mark.*

The Secretary's statement regarding the cradle at the time of the Pharaohs, however, appears to be inaccurate, as it was not invented until about 200 years ago.

When we consider the marvelous food we have available for our table, we should not forget the contribution which the Indians made: corn, sweet potatoes, tomatoes, pumpkins, gourds, squashes, watermelons, beans, grapes, berries, pecans, black walnuts, peanuts, maple sugar, geese, ducks, white potatoes, turkeys, according to the chronology referred to in the footnote.

During the first century B.C., Cicero in his "Essay On Old Age" wrote enthusiastically of farm life at a time when it must have been much more onerous than it was sixty to seventy years ago:

> I come now to the pleasures of the farmer, in which I take amazing delight. These are not hindered by any extent of old age, and seem to me to approach nearest to the ideal wise man's life. For he has to deal with the earth, which never refuses its obedience, nor ever returns what it has received without usury; sometimes, indeed, with less, but generally with greater interest. For my part, however, it is not merely the thing produced, but the earth's own force and natural productiveness that delight me. For having received in its bosom the seed scattered broadcast upon it, softened and broken up, she first keeps it concealed therein (hence the harrowing which accomplishes this gets its name from a word meaning 'to hide'); next, when it has been warmed by her heat and close pressure, she splits it open and draws from it the greenery of the blade. This, supported by the fibres of the root, little by little grows up, and held upright by its jointed stalk is enclosed in sheaths, as being still immature. When it has emerged from them it produces an ear of

*See Department of Agriculture's *Chronology of American Agriculture, 1790–1973; Land of Plenty,* by Land Equipment Institute; *McCormick Reaper Centennial Source Material;* and Oaklay's *Man The Toolmaker,* published by the British Museum.

corn arranged in order, and is defended against the pecking of the smaller birds by a regular palisade of spikes.*

Cicero was referring to corn in its generic sense, which includes wheat and other small grains, and not to our native Indian corn, which was unknown to Europe prior to the time of the English settlements in this country.

*From "Letters and Treatises of Cicero and Pliny" in *Harvard Classics* (New York: P.E. Collier & Son, 1909), IX:45,63-64.

CHAPTER SEVEN

The Country Woman

EMERSON SAID THAT a beautiful woman was a practical poet, taming her savage mate, planting tenderness, hope and eloquence in all whom she approached; that she was a part of nature, mixing her form with the moon and the stars, with the woods and the waters; that she filled man's vase with wine and roses to the brim; and that when she was around, the years swift-winged and unnoticed fled away.

Neither Emerson nor other poets seemed to have had in mind the country woman, for she was forced to lead a more utilitarian life. Around the turn of the century, the farmer's wife was as indispensable to successful farming as the farmer himself. There probably was no other business or profession in which the cooperation of husband and wife was as important as in agriculture.

While the men were in the barn early in the morning feeding the teams and the cattle, the women were busy preparing breakfast and making up the beds. Country meals required substantial food, full of carbohydrates and protein, to provide the brawn and stamina needed for heavy farm work. Consequently, ham, bacon, sausage, eggs, biscuits, cornbread, pancakes, molasses, butter, milk and coffee made up the breakfast menu.

After breakfast the distaff members of the family washed the dishes and swept the floors. During the next few hours, they were engaged in baking bread, sewing buttons and patches on old clothes, cutting and making new clothing, knitting mittens and sweaters, working in the garden and orchard, picking and canning fruit, depending upon the season.

Dinner came in the middle of the day, not at its end. During the summer, the men were called from the field about noon by the ringing of a copper bell on the top of a high post, or by the blowing of a conchshell used as a horn. They watered and fed the teams, then sat down at the table shortly after noon. Dinner sometimes included pie and cake.

After dinner the men took a short siesta, lying on the floor before returning to the field to resume their work. In the meantime, the women washed the dishes, then enjoyed a short respite from their household duties before taking up their various chores.

In the late afternoon, the family dog rounded up the cows and drove them in from the pasture. Although the men sometimes did the milking in the morning, the women always did it in the evening. Milking was performed by sitting on a three-legged stool and squeezing the milk out of the cow's udder into a pail on the ground.

When the ritual was over, the milk was stored in jars and crocks in the underground cellar until it was used for drinking, cooking, making butter or ice cream. The cellar usually was simply a hole dug in the ground near the kitchen. It was about six feet deep, eight feet wide, and twelve feet long. The roof was constructed of rafters and boards, which were overlaid with dirt covered with sod. Even during the driest and hottest weather, an underground cellar provided satisfactory refrigeration for dairy products and fresh fruits and vegetables.

The last item on the women's agenda was preparing supper and washing the dishes, but they sometimes busied themselves with sewing and knitting until time to go to bed.

In addition, certain work was done on special days. Monday was washday. The clothes were scrubbed by hand by rubbing them up and down over a corrugated washboard placed in a zinc tub of warm cistern water. Rainwater was used, as it was softer and more susceptible to sudsiness than water from the well. Following the washing, the clothes were hand-rinsed in a tub of clear water, then hung on the clothesline in the yard to dry. The next day, they were ironed and placed in the bureau drawers.

One day a week was set aside for making butter. The "cream in a golden languor slept" until it was ready to be skimmed off the milk. It was put in a cylindrical wooden cask made of staves and bound with metal bands. Inside the cask was a round perforated-disc agitator. This was attached to the bottom of the wooden handle which protruded through a hole in the middle of the lid on the top of the churn. Churning consisted of moving the handle up and down in a fast motion until the butter was separated from the milk, which became buttermilk.

Now and then, cottage cheese was made by allowing the milk to curdle, placing the clabber inside a cheesecloth, and squeezing out the whey.

One of the most satisfactory aspects of early country life was the cooperation of the neighbors at the log-rollings, hog-killings and wheat-threshings. When these community affairs occurred, the wives and daughters of the neighborhood cooperated in preparing large banquet-type dinners and suppers. The tables invariably were overladen with meats, fried and stewed chicken and dumplings, vegetables, fruits, cakes and pies. In those pre-liberation days, the women always waited on the table, while the men enjoyed the feast. They themselves did not partake of the repast until after the men had finished. At the wheat threshings, which occurred during the summer, one or two women fanned the flies away from the table with a homemade fan of paper strips or stringers fastened to a small pole about five feet long.

Country women also found time to weave carpets for the floors. They used a four-poster loom about eight feet long, five feet wide, and six feet high, with a wooden bench at the front. Colored yarns or threads known as warp were wound around the revolving beam at the back, brought forward in parallel lines through a midway harness or heddle, and fastened to a small rotary beam at the front.

The loom was operated by pressing a foot-treadle to which the heddle was attached. This caused the alternate warp threads to be raised and the complementary ones to be lowered simultaneously, thus forming a shed between the intersection of the upper and the lower yarns. Narrow strips of colored cloth or rags, called woof, were fastened to a shuttle and passed to and fro by hand through the shed. At the end of each shuttling, the foot-treadle was pressed down, causing the heddle to depress the upper and to elevate the lower threads and hence, to make a new shed for the next passing of the shuttle. Simultaneously, the woof was battened firmly into the weave behind the intersection of the threads. As the work progressed, the warp threads were unwound from the cylinder in the rear and the woven carpet was wound around the rotary beam in the front. Weaving sufficient yardage sometimes required two or three years, as there was precious little time for it.

Quilting was another extra-curricular activity of farm women. At times they cooperated, and at other times they worked alone. A variety of colored cloths were cut into irregular patches and sewed into crazy-quilt patterns a few inches square. When a sufficient number of these patterns were finished, they were stitched together to form the fancy covering for the top of the quilt. The next step was to fasten the lower backing material to a wooden frame to hold it in a taut position. Then, cotton batting was placed over it, and the variegated patchwork was placed on top and fastened to the frame. The quilt was finished by stitching the backing, the cotton and the cover together with threads or yarns. The final result was a decorative crazy quilt coverlet for the bed. These early pieces now command good to high prices.

What can one say of the life of the country woman some seventy to eighty years ago? That it was a life of drudgery cannot be denied. Her work started early in the morning and lasted well into the night. The old aphorism, "A woman's work is never done," must have originated in the country. It is doubtful whether one in a hundred ever received a present on her birthday or at any other time; nor did she expect any. Luxuries were not a part of the country woman's life. Despite these hardships, she seemed to be contented and willingly gave her all to her family. Usually, she was rewarded with the deep respect and gratitude which her sacrifices inspired.

One who spent his early days in the country around the turn of the century is bound to have a feeling of remorse, when he recalls the hardships that his mother and sisters, as well as all other farm women, suffered. He wishes that their lives could have been easier, and that the brief periods of joy and respite could have been expanded. Of course, nothing could have been done, as it was the custom of the age. Even then, their lives were much easier than those of the pioneer women one hundred years before, when the pioneers were carving their homes out of the wilderness.

Remembrance of our mother brings back many fond memories. She was kind, soft-spoken, patient and self-effacing. She listened to others and talked very little herself. During our tender years, she was a solace to us. Remembrance of her now is like a continuous flow of love down through the vista of the years. My three sisters were cast in a similar mold. Regrettably, we lost our oldest sister prematurely in her prime.

One can agree with the German Poet A.C. Friedrich Schiller:

> Honor to women! They twine and weave the roses of Heaven into the life of man. It is they that unite us in the fascinating bonds of love. Concealed in the modest veil of the graces, they cherish carefully the external fire of delicate feeling with holy hands.

CHAPTER EIGHT

The Country School

OUR SCHOOL, KNOWN as the Downen School, was a one-room red brick schoolhouse situated on an acre of ground immediately south of the graveyard on the ancestral farm. A bell on top of the facade end was rung at the beginning of school, at noon, at the morning and afternoon recesses, and at the parting school day. Two frame outhouses and a coal shed behind the schoolhouse and a cistern at the side completed the complex.

School began early in September and ended about the middle of May. Some thirty pupils attended during the winter. The number during the spring and fall usually was smaller, due to the necessity of some of the boys' staying home to work on the farm. Pupils walked to school over the dirt roads, as far as three or four miles in good weather. During rainy or snowy days, they sometimes were carried in buggies, wagons or sleds.

Coats, overshoes and lunch boxes were placed on shelves in the vestibule at the front end of the schoolhouse. The teacher's desk was on a dais at the back of the room. The recitation seats faced the teacher's desk. Behind them were the double seats and desks occupied by the eight grades. The only illumination was the daylight coming through the three windows on each side of the schoolroom.

A pot-bellied coal stove occupied a spot in the middle of the room. On cold winter days, it became red-hot, practically roasting everyone sitting nearby. Blackboards and slates were used, as well as pencils and paper.

School opened at nine in the morning and closed at half-past four in the afternoon. One teacher taught all eight grades. The first period during the morning was devoted to reciting the Lord's Prayer and singing patriotic and other songs.

The subjects taught were reading, arithmetic, spelling, physiology, grammar, history, geography, penmanship and German. The latter was for the benefit of the German children, who predominated in the region, although anyone else could study the language if he desired.

For their classes, the pupils went to the recitation seats in front of the teacher's desk. Recitations usually were limited to fifteen minutes. As soon as one ended, another began. Under these circumstances, the only time available for study was while other pupils were reciting their lessons.

Fifteen-minute recesses in mid-morning and mid-afternoon and an hour intermission at noon were given over to play and exercise. The games were somewhat similar to those of today, except no fixed athletic equipment was provided. One of the games of that period is probably unknown today. Two teams took positions on opposite sides of the schoolhouse, and a ball was thrown over the roof, back and forth, until a member of one of the teams caught it. The team catching the ball yelled "andy-over" and sallied forth to the other side, some going around one way and the others skirting the opposite end of the schoolhouse. The game was to hit a member of the other team with the ball and force him to change sides.

Although the teacher was kept busy continuously with classes, discipline in the school was fortunately never the problem it was later to become in permissive times. There was no loitering in the corridor or outside of the schoolroom, while school was in session. "Spare the rod and spoil the child" had not come into vogue. The teacher kept a cane handy and did not scruple to use it to maintain order, as an experience of my own amply demonstrates. While I was holding a lead pencil in front of my eyes and sighting down it in simulation of aiming a gun, the schoolmarm, much to my surprise and chagrin, suddenly struck it out of my hands with a bang onto the floor. She accomplished this *tour de force* with a pointer, which she invariably carried in her hand. I would not have dreamed of protesting her action.

Another teacher, one of our best, gave a boy a sound caning, which most of us felt he richly deserved. But his father did not approve and took his son out of school. This episode had repercussions. While the teacher was working in the wheat field at threshing time during the next summer, the father attacked him in retaliation for the whipping administered to his son. In the fight, the father was bested and given a good thrashing himself. He, in turn, had his revenge later by preventing the reappointment of the teacher at the Downen School.

Strange how minor incidents from the distant past sometimes crop out of one's subconscious mind. I well recall one that occurred about eighty years ago, when I picked up a dead broken limb of a tree in the nearby woods at recess and hurled it at a bird sitting on the branch of a small bush. It was not my intention to harm the bird; but much to my surprise, the stick struck it down dead in the snow. John Wollman, an itinerant Quaker preacher along the Eastern seaboard during the middle of eighteenth century, recorded a similar incident in his journal:

> In my childhood, on going to a neighbor's house, I saw on the way a robin sitting on her nest, and as I came near she went off; but having some young ones, she flew about and with many cries expressed her concern for them. I stood and threw stones at her and, one striking her, she fell down dead. At first, I was pleased with my exploit, but after a few minutes was seized with horror at having in a sportive way killed an innocent creature while she was caring for her young.*

Only a few social events took place at the Downen School, of which two may be worthy of notice.

In the fall, a box supper was held in the schoolhouse at night for the benefit of the school library. As there was no artificial lighting, it was necessary to use lanterns. Girls from the nearby farms brought boxes for two to be auctioned to the highest bidders. A

---

*From "The Journal of John Wollman" in *Harvard Classics* (New York: P.E. Collier & Son, 1916), III:845.

farmer acted as auctioneer. The bidding became pretty spirited when some of the swains bid up the price of the box of the best girl of one of the other boys. After the boxes were sold, the suppers were enjoyed by the girls and the lucky bidders. The prices ranged from fifty cents to a dollar a box, and the total intake usually amounted to $20.00 to $25.00.

Exercises were held at the beginning of the Christmas season and at the close of school. Parents were invited to hear their children sing, recite poetry and monologues. The teacher usually gave the pupils a present at Christmas, which usually was a small bag of candy, paid for out of her own purse.

Around 1900, we ceremoniously planted trees on Arbor Day. The ones selected were small sugar maples, which we dug up in the nearby woods and transplanted on each side of the schoolhouse. We were told that sugar maples sometimes lived to be up to 500 years old; that about ten percent of the wood of a tree is underground in the form of roots; that the function of the roots is to anchor the tree firmly into the ground and to provide it with air, minerals and water; and that the roots of some trees at maturity would extend for several miles, if they were stretched out end to end.

A well-deserved tribute to a tree is a notice in a park in Portugal:

> To ye who would pass by and raise your hand against me, harken ere you harm me. I am the heat of your hearth on the cold winter nights; the friendly shade screening you from the summer sun; and my fruits are refreshing draughts quenching your thirst as you journey on. I am the beam that holds your house, the board of your table, the bed on which you lie, and the timber that builds your boat. I am the handle of your hoe, the door of your homestead, the wood of your cradle, and the shell of your coffin. I am the gift of God and the friend of man.

Around the turn of the century, few country boys continued their education beyond the eighth grade, either from lack of ambition or want of means. Indeed, most discontinued school even before they finished the lower grades, as there were then no state laws demanding attendance. Most of the farmers and their wives had obtained very scanty schooling, and it may have been that they felt that what was good enough for them was good enough for their children.

My experience seems to have been an exception, as it was my good fortune to break away from this country habit and to attend high school at Wadesville. My father and mother were insistent that their children should have a better education than they themselves had been able to receive.

Wadesville was about five miles from home, and usually I rode there by horse. If all the horses were busy on the farm, I had to walk. I also have a vivid recollection of skating to school over the ice-covered roads and fields, after the major icestorm of 1900.

The Village of Wadesville was made up of about 75 people. The high school occupied the upstairs room of a frame building, the lower floor being used by the grade school. Its thirty or forty students lived in the village and on nearby farms. A single teacher, a graduate of Indiana University, taught the usual high school subjects of Latin, algebra, geometry, history, English, composition and civics.

The County Superintendent of Schools was elected by the voters of Posey County for a term of four years. He had supervision of the public schools, with headquarters in Mt. Vernon, the county seat. He made an effort to visit each of the country schools every year, making his rounds with a horse and buggy. Every year the superintendent gave written examinations to applicants for teachers' licenses.

As a result of such an examination during my sixteenth year, I was granted a one-year's license to teach in 1902. The second year, a three-year's license was issued to me, the highest license at that time.

The trustee of my township gave me a position at the Downen School at a salary of forty dollars per month. School was an eight-months period, so my total salary for the year was $320.00. Out of this it was necessary for me to pay one of the boys ten cents a day to sweep the floor and to start the fire in the morning, or to do it myself.

Some of the pupils, who were schoolmates at the time of my

leaving for Wadesville High School, now came under my tutelage, so it is not surprising that a few of them tried to test my mettle. The most trying incident was when one of the boys drew a knife on me in school. I immediately grabbed him by his shoulders and gave him such a violent shaking that his knife was flung from his grasp and his desk was heaved from the floor. He was sent home, where he received further chastisement. When he returned to school, he was more amenable to discipline. This episode seemed to have a salutary effect, as no other major breach of discipline occurred during the time I was teaching at Downen School.

By that enlightened year the dunce cap was out of vogue; but the punishment for minor infractions of the rules was much the same. Guilty pupils were required to stand near the teacher's desk sans the cap and face the entire student body—which smirked, when teacher wasn't looking, at the humiliated one. This happened very seldom, as everyone understood that he was there for study.

Teachers before me, as well as I, played the games on the playground with the pupils as one of themselves. When the recess was over, the teacher resumed his role as teacher and disciplinarian, and students were not allowed to take advantage of the earlier informalities.

Country schoolteachers were required to attend the County Institutes in Mt. Vernon during the early fall before school began and also the Township Institutes, once each month. The Township Trustee usually was present at the latter and paid us our monthly salaries and an additional stipend of five dollars for attending the Institute.

Teachers rotated in presiding at the Township Institutes and in leading the discussions. Most had several years of experience, so it was with some diffidence that I, as a novice, took over when my turn came.

Various subjects were discussed at our Township Institutes. Two new books were published about 1900, which we studied in considerable detail: Nicolay and Hay's *Abraham Lincoln,* and Lockwood's *New Harmony Movement.* These books were of special interest to Posey County teachers, as Lincoln had lived from 1816 to 1830 at Gentryville, Indiana, about forty miles away, and New Harmony, site of the religious and communistic experiments of the Rappites and the socialistic and educational ventures of the Owenites during the early decades of the nineteenth century, was located in Posey County itself.

Indiana teachers also were required to attend the Indiana State Normal School at Terre Haute during its summer sessions. In addition to the credits for the courses taken, I was granted eleven credits for my three years' license. The Normal had only two buildings at the time, and the tuition amounted to two dollars per term for the use of the library. The costs of board and room were only a few dollars per week.

CHAPTER NINE

The Country Church

AROUND THE TURN of the century some thirty churches were located in the Posey County countryside: General Baptists, Regular Baptists, Methodists, Lutherans, Presbyterians and Catholics. Baptists and Lutherans predominated. Most of the churches were near schoolhouses, and as a rule they were white, one-room, frame buildings with a belfry at the front end. Wood and coal pot-bellied stoves heated them during the wintertime, and long, straight-backed wooden benches were used as pews. The Mt. Zion and Mt. Pleasant Churches, two General Baptist churches near our home, also had a mourners' bench near the altar. Those moved by the message repaired there to repent, pray and confess their sins.

None of the country preachers, except possibly the Catholic and Lutheran, ever had been a seminarian. They were self-educated in lay as well as in ecclesiastical matters. But this did not detract from their knowledge of the Bible. They were avid biblical students and so earnest and forceful in delivering their messages that they sometimes were known as "exhorters." Fundamentalists, they believed in the literal interpretation of the Scriptures. Their sermons were devoted to "old-time religion" and were devoid of any secular reference to civil rights, politics, or other controversial subjects. They were the *vox dei* in the interpretation of the Bible and not the *vox populi* in the exposition of the Constitution.

Due to their intensive study, country preachers were able to quote long passages from the Scriptures. William Jackson

Blackburn, my maternal grandfather, was a General Baptist preacher, and I recall with a sense of embarrassment how he used to quiz me regarding some of the most important passages from Genesis to Revelations.

My grandfather was a veteran of the Civil War, a member of an Indiana regiment that fought at the Battle of Shiloh near the Tennessee-Mississippi border along the Mississippi River in April, 1862. A bullet from the rifle of a Southern soldier grazed his left temple and felled him. It has occurred to me that if this bullet had been a faction of an inch farther to the left, he would not have lived to tell me, nor would I have been here to relate the anecdote. For his service in the Northern army, my grandfather received the munificent pension of thirty dollars a month.

Some of these country preachers, especially those of the General Baptist and Methodist denominations, travelled the circuit in the southwestern part of Indiana and nearby sections of Kentucky and Illinois. They usually made the trip by train, if the distance were long, and by horse and buggy, if it were short.

Sunday school and prayer meetings were held every Sunday, and regular church services were conducted on Saturday and Sunday once each month. A minister's pay rarely exceeded fifteen dollars a month. In addition, he usually was entertained by the members in their homes during his pastoral visits.

Revival meetings of two or three weeks' duration were held during the winter to rekindle interest in the congregation and to increase membership. Sometimes the regular pastor conducted these services. At other times, a specialist in revivals was engaged to preach. Members of other congregations throughout the county often attended these revivals and swelled the attendance, as this was one form of emotional expression not frowned upon as trivial or unholy.

A good evangelist had a powerful influence over the congregation. His sermons sometimes were so impassioned, zealous and forceful that the members practically trembled as his voice rose to a pitch of righteous indignation. Everyone found himself face to face with his own conscience. Some became excited; some sobbed and shook with contrition and remorse; others sat as if awaiting their doom. Some who had been sobbing and weeping suddenly cried aloud with joyful ejaculations of "Amen! Amen!" "Fools, who came to scoff, remained to pray." Brought face to face with their ungodly living, they were converted and confessed their sins—generally, to backslide a bit, according to human nature. But that was for future revival meetings to deal with.

An old story tells of an evangelist who was engaged to conduct revival services in a country church. He told the parishioners that he would answer any questions regarding the Bible they might present. One night after he had finished his exhortations, a young man arose in the congregation and held up his hand. The preacher awaited the question.

"The Bible says that only two people were created by God, Adam and Eve, and that they had two sons, Cain and Abel. Cain slew Abel and was banished to the Land of Nod, where he took unto himself a wife. Can you explain whose daughter was Cain's wife?"

For a moment, the evangelist was nonplussed, but soon he recovered his composure.

"Young man," he said, "just keep your mind on your own troubles, and keep it off other men's wives."

Farmers took their families to church in a buggy, surrey or wagon, tethering their horses to the hitching posts in the church-yard. Services ordinarily lasted at least two hours, consisting of congregational singing, praying, reading the Scriptures and the sermon. At that time, there was no choir or organ in the General Baptist churches. Most of the members were convinced that instrumental music was the tool of the devil in the church as well as in the dance hall.

The church was a social as well as a religious institution. It afforded country people about the only opportunity they had to get together in groups and visit with one another. It was the custom of the men to stay outside the meeting house before and after services and discuss farming conditions, the weather and the news, while the women usually did their visiting inside the church.

Church dinners during the summertime provided another pleasant social relaxation. The farmers' wives prepared enormous quantities of food at home which they took to the church, where it was served on long wooden tables under the churchyard trees.

The Baptists believed in baptism by complete submersion under the water. Converts were baptized in Big Creek, in ponds on the farms, and· in the Ohio and Wabash Rivers, sometimes in water muddied by recent rains, just as Christ was baptized in the River Jordan by John the Baptist. During a visit to Old Jericho and the Dead Sea a few years ago, I was surprised to learn that the Jordan was not much larger than Big Creek in Posey County.

When country folks died, they were laid to rest in the graveyard adjoining the church. The funeral procession started at the home of the deceased and plodded along the unpaved road to the church. Sometimes the cortege was a half-mile or more in length—the buggies, surreys, and wagons following the horse-drawn hearse. The funeral sermon was preached inside the church, after which the deceased was entombed in the churchyard.

> As the long train
> Of ages glides away, the sons of man,
> The youth in life's green spring, and he who goes
> In the full strength of years—matron, and maid,
> And the sweet babe, and the gray-headed man—
> Shall one by one be gathered to thy side,
> By those, who in their turn shall follow them.

> *Thanatopsis*
> William Cullen Bryant

While visiting the Palace Ga' Renzoneco alongside the Grand Canal in Venice, where Robert Browning lived for twenty-eight years, I was reminded of the theme of Bryant's famous poem on reading the epitaph on the tomb of a member of the Venetian family buried there:

"Where you are, we were; where we are, you will be."

CHAPTER TEN

The Country Village

THE NEAREST VILLAGE to our farm was Oliver Station. It was west of Big Creek on the C. & E. I. Railroad about halfway between Fort Branch and Mt. Vernon, and about three miles from home. Its population of thirty or forty people lived in small frame houses. There was a country store, dance hall, barber shop, saloon, blacksmith shop and doctor. In addition to groceries and dry goods, the storekeeper sold women's and men's clothing, tools and kitchen ware. He bought chickens, eggs, and butter from farm women for cash or traded store goods to them in barter. During the summer, he sometimes took his wares to the country in a horse-drawn huckster's wagon and picked up produce at the farms. He also was agent in buying wheat and corn from farmers.

Before the inauguration of Rural Free Delivery of the mail in 1902, the storekeeper was the Oliver postmaster. When the farmers went to Oliver for their mail, they took their produce to him for sale and bought store goods from him.

Occasional dances were held in the hall above the store. Boys and girls from the farms and neighboring villages came to dance the waltz and the square dance to the tunes of two violins and a bass fiddle, and the rhythm of the fiddlers' feet on the floor. The musicians played by ear. The square dance was more popular than the waltz. Boys took their girls to the dances by horse and buggy or simply by walking along the country roads. It was the custom of the boys to wear linen dusters in the summertime, if they were lucky enough to have a buggy.

The barber relied chiefly upon farming and broom-making for a living, doing his barbering chiefly on Saturdays, especially when dances were held. To make the best impression on his girl friend, the male escort would get a haircut and a shave. A shave cost ten cents and haircut twenty to twenty-five cents.

The village store and the barber shop were favorite places for men to congregate, tell jokes, and discuss politics and the news. They sat around the potbellied stove on boxes, kegs and chairs and used a box of ashes for a cuspidor, which they could spot most of the time, no matter how far away it was. A great deal of razzing one another took place; but it never developed beyond the friendly stage.

Especially on Saturday nights, the saloon came in for its share of business. There was very little drunkenness; however, now and then a customer imbibed too freely and became so inebriated that he had to be taken home.

The blacksmith shod the horses and mules, sharpened the plowshares, and did all other kinds of metalwork for the farming community.

In "The Village Blacksmith" Longfellow described the smithy:*

> The smith a mighty man is he
> With large and sinewy hands,
> And the muscles of his brawny arms
> Are as strong as iron bands.

He developed this strength by pumping the handle of a bellows to fan the forge and by wielding a heavy blacksmith's hammer to beat the red-hot horseshoes and plowshares into shape.

In shoeing a horse, the smithy lifted one of its feet off the ground. He held it firmly between his upper legs, while he trimmed the bottom of the hoof with a flexible knife and smoothed it with a coarse file. Then he dropped the foot to the ground, grasped a

---

*From *Favorite Poems of Henry Wadsworth Longfellow* (Garden City, New York: International Collectors Library), pp. 323–325. Introduction and illustrations copyrighted 1947 by Doubleday and Company.

horseshoe with a pair of long tongs, and thrust it into the hot coals of the forge. He fanned the fire by pumping the bellows, which forced the air up from underneath the flaming coals of the furnace. When the shoe was red-hot, he placed it on the anvil and hammered it into the shape of the horse's hoof. The sparks scintillated in every direction, some striking against his leathern apron before falling onto the dirt floor.

The next step was to place the hot shoe in a wooden tub of water to sizzle, and be tempered. He then lifted the horse's foot up again to see if the shoe would fit the hoof. If it did not, the smithy heated and smote it some more until it had the proper shape.

Finally, the shoe was fastened to the hoof with horseshoe nails, which stuck through the outside of the wall. They were nipped off near the surface with a pair of pincers. The jagged ends were bent over with a small hammer, and the hoof was filed to give it a smooth finish. Usually, the two front feet were shod; but sometimes the two rear ones also were covered.

During the summer and fall, flies were such a nuisance that it was necessary to fan them away from the horses while they were being shod. This chore usually fell to a farmboy, who switched the pests with a small bush or other makeshift fan, and was glad to do it, just to watch this always interesting procedure.

The steel plowshares and colters were dulled by constantly cutting into the roots of the stumps. Periodically, they were taken to the blacksmith's shop. The smith heated them red hot, then hammered the dull edges on the anvil until they were thin and sharp, tempering the steel by gradually cooling it in the tub of water.

The brittle cast-iron plowshares could not be sharpened in this manner. The smithy used a foot treadle to rotate an emery wheel and held the dull edges against it until they were smooth and sharp. All the while sparks flew fast and furiously in every direction onto the floor.

One never tired of lingering and loitering and watching the jagged blazes popping out of the forge and the red-hot sparks scintillating from the anvil and emery wheel.

The local doctor maintained a small frame office in the yard of his home across the road from the store. He kept two or three horses, as he frequently needed a fresh one during a busy day or night. He fed, curried and harnessed them himself. He called upon his country patients by different means, in good weather by a two-wheeled, one-horse cart; in bad weather, by horseback with his medical supplies in his saddle bag; in snowy weather, sometimes in a sled. During extremely dark nights, he frequently carried a lantern to light the way along the country roads.

Before the advent of the party telephone around 1900, it sometimes was necessary for me to ride a horse to Oliver to ask the doctor to make a call. Frequently the road was so slippery that my mount had difficulty in keeping on his feet. The road led down a mile-long hill to Big Creek, across the wooden bridge, and through the woody bottoms on the far side. The hooting of the owls lamenting during the nighttime, the barking of the foxes, and the glow of the *ignis-fatuus* created a strange, eerie feeling in me as I wended my way along the winding road to Oliver.

On one occasion after crossing the bridge, my horse snorted, stopped short and pitched me over the pommel of the saddle bow onto his maney neck. He stood still long enough for me to sit back on the saddle and make a reconnaisance. About fifty yards up the side of the road in front of us, a coon stood with its fiery eyes flashing in the moonlight. Soon, it retreated into the adjoining woods and my mount recovered its composure sufficiently for us to continue.

The doctor never failed to respond to a call, winter or summer, rain or shine, day or night, even though he knew that the patient might be unable to pay him. He never sent a bill, either, but relied on voluntary payments. He spent a great deal of time studying his patients and comforting them. He always took his powders and pills with him, as there was no drugstore in which a prescription could be filled within a distance of several miles. He treated all kinds of ailments—itch, sore throat, tapeworms, uremic poisoning, warts, eczema, boils, toothaches, headaches, and colds and fevers. He set broken bones, and in emergencies he shaped splints from pieces of wood with his own knife and used bedsheets and wadding from old quilts for paddings. For stiff joints and other similar troubles, he used hot bags of flaxseed to bring the blood to the surface. As there were no hospitals in the region, he brought babies into the world in the homes with no other antiseptic than soap and hot water.

The village doctor's fees were extremely small, ranging from "four-bits" or fifty cents, for office calls to a dollar for home calls, depending upon the distance from his office. The customary charge for delivering a baby was ten dollars.

The country doctor is indeed one of the unsung heroes of past generations.

Oliver Station was the meeting place of country and village boys on Sundays and holidays, where we pitched silver dollars and horeshoes, shot marbles, played baseball and indulged in boxing. Many a Sunday and holiday we walked four or five miles from home to take part in these games, and at the end of the day we trudged back again for another week's work on the farm.

The goals in pitching dollars were two small holes slightly larger than a silver dollar, dug in the ground about twenty-five feet apart. The players stood behind the holes and each in turn pitched his dollar at the opposite hole.

For the game of marbles, a circle was drawn on the ground and a dozen or so marbles were placed inside. The player shot his taw, which sometimes was an agate, from the tawline, some fifteen to twenty feet away at the marbles in the ring. As long as he knocked a marble out of the circle, he continued to shoot. When he missed, the next player began at the tawline. The one who dislodged the most marbles won the game.

Two kinds of games were played, one in which the player held his hand in the air and the other in which he held his knuckle on the ground to make the shot. Occasionally, a player became so expert that he could blast a marble out of the ring and leave his taw spinning in the exact spot occupied by the displaced marble.

Another game was "mumblety-peg." Two blades of a knife were opened, one parallel and the other perpendicular with the handle.

The knife was held in different positions, either on the ground or in the air, and flipped end-over-end. The knife could come to rest with the perpendicular or the parallel blade, or both sticking into the ground. Certain points were assigned to the different positions. The winner pressed a wooden peg lightly into the ground with his thumb, closed his eyes, and struck at it with the back of his knife. The loser was required to pull the peg out of the ground with his teeth. Needless to say, if the winner was lucky in hitting the peg, the situation for the loser was unpleasant.

None of the boys exhibited any special professionalism in boxing. They did indulge in some strenuous fisticuffs and provided entertainment for the older men, who egged them on. Once a parvenu came to Oliver and wielded the gloves so cleverly that everyone looked upon him as the champion—until one of the local boys landed such a stiff uppercut to his jaw that the newcomer instantly threw in the sponge, and faith in our local ability at self-defense was restored.

Baseball was the game in which the greatest dexterity was demonstrated. The playing field was a pasture near the doctor's office. To maintain interest in the sport, the games were rotated among the different villages.

The shortline railroad running through Oliver Station held a special attraction for country youth. We could hear the clanging of the wheels pounding the rails, the tolling of the bell, and the shrill noise of the whistle. We could see the banner of steam floating behind the locomotive and glistening in the sunlight, as it came racing down the railroad tracks, throbbing and panting into the station, and we could also wish we could respond to the conductor's "All aboard!"

The train always stopped to discharge freight and passengers, pick up a box car loaded with wheat or corn, or leave an empty one to be loaded and taken away later on. Unless it was flagged, it never stopped solely to take on passengers. The conductor and engineer seemed to carry a sort of aura about them, as they were going places, while we were mere spectators staying home. We often wondered whether we might be going somewhere ourselves, when we were at last on our own.

The section handcar was, next to the train itself, of special interest. The railroad was kept in a state of repair by section hands who operated the car by pushing down and pulling up on double parallel handlebars with their hands. As the car ran on the railroad tracks, it picked up considerable speed taking the section hands to and from their places of work and carrying their tools.

The railroad was not as romantic in the eyes of the farmers, however, especially those living alongside the track. The trains sometimes killed their livestock that wandered onto the tracks, caused their teams to run away, and demolished their buggies and wagons stalled on the crossings. These accidents always provoked antagonisms, and sometimes they resulted in lawsuits in the county court at Mt. Vernon.

Going to Oliver Station on Sundays and holidays was one of the highlights of a country boy's life. It mitigated the loneliness of isolation and broke the monotony of farm work. In fact, these respites were about the only vacations one ever had from the farm, except a trip in a buggy or wagon to Mt. Vernon or Evansville.

There was an exception to this custom in the case of two other boys and myself. In 1904, we were permitted to go to the World's Fair in St. Louis, which was held in celebration of the Louisiana Purchase of 1803. Packing our scanty clothing in our flimsy suitcases, we took the coach on the L. & N. Railroad from Mt. Vernon to St. Louis. As this was our first trip away from home, there was not a little apprehension on our part about visiting such a large city. We were familiar with the Wabash, which soon was behind us; but the Father of Waters to us was a mere serpentine line on a map in our geography book. In the course of a few hours, we passed over the mighty Mississippi on the long steel bridge.

Naturally, we acted our part as rustics in a big city, for we could not very well do otherwise. We knew nothing about hotels or other lodging places, so we took a streetcar in search of a room. On the way, one of our suitcases fell apart and scattered everything all over the aisle of the car. Finally, we found a room for about a dollar a day and proceeded to take in the fair.

One of my purchases was a "gold watch" to use in teaching school. It turned out to be brass. We made a visit to a large room containing a maze of mirrors, reminiscent of the labyrinth at Knossus in which Theseus attacked and slew the Minotaur.

We took an excursion boat up the Mississippi to Hannibal, Missouri, the old home of Mark Twain. As we approached the mouth of the Missouri, it was discharging its muddy waters into the Mississippi and discoloring the course of the latter for several miles downstream.

Needless to say, we were the talk of the country, after we returned home from our excursion to the big city.

CHAPTER ELEVEN

Country Customs and Hobbies

FEW MANUFACTURED toys were for sale at the beginning of this century, especially in small country towns. Farm children had to do without or exercise their ingenuity in making their own. Boys fashioned sleds from thick boards, slingshots out of forked twigs and wide bands of rubber, popguns and squirtguns out of hollow sections of elderberry bushes, ramrods from seasoned oak wood, bows out of hickory sprouts and strong cords, and arrows from dead weeds and slivers of dry, light wood. Sometimes an arrow was capped with a thin, flint arrowhead found on the farm. Girls made their dolls out of rags and doll dresses from pieces of cloth.

During the fall and winter, rabbit hunting was a country pastime. Rabbits were as wily as a fox in weaving, zigzagging, backtracking and jumping sideways into another rabbit's track to throw a dog or other pursuer off its own track. When in its nest, it was well camouflaged within its gray and white surroundings. Even its flashy cottontail was hidden. It would make only three imprints with its four feet, bringing down its two hind feet together so as to make a single track.

Some writers have indulged in a bit of speculation as to the use a rabbit makes of its cottontail. Some say it is flashed as a lure to its pursuing predators to keep down its population. Others say it flips its tail from side to side to fool its pursuers into believing that it is changing its course, when in fact it is continuing on a straight line.

The usual way of hunting rabbits was with a shotgun. Bows and arrows also were used. One seldom had any luck with this method, which was too slow, unless he were a good archer and able to find a rabbit ensconced snugly in its nest. Homemade traps sometimes were tried, made of slim strips of wood and a box. One strip about ten inches long was posted upright on the ground, another slightly longer was placed in a longitudinal position a few inches above the ground, and another formed the diagonal. The three pieces were held together in the form of a right-angled triangle by means of notches cut into their sides. A box with a weight on top was placed over the trap, with one end resting on the ground and the other on the apex of the triangle. An apple or other bait was stuck on the end of the horizontal stick inside the box. Rabbits were pretty cagy, though, and rarely if ever nibbled on the bait. If one did, the trap would collapse like a stack of cards and hold it captive until taken out.

Squirrel hunting was a fall and winter sport, when the corn was in ear and acorns, walnuts and hickory nuts were on the trees. Squirrel hunting extended into spring and early summer, when the mulberries were ripe. The best hunting time was after a rain, when the mists were slowly lifting and the leaves were wet. One could move noiselessly through the undergrowth without being seen or heard. Sometimes, a half-dozen or more squirrels would be gambolling or feasting on a single tree. Returning home from hunting one morning in 1901, I learned of the assassination of President McKinley, and I always associate those two events in my memory.

Coon hunting was a nocturnal sport during the late fall and winter, when the leaves were off the trees. The best place was in Big Creek Bottoms. A good dog could track a coon by its scent until it climbed a tree, usually a white oak or tulip poplar. While a dog was trailing the coon, we could follow the course of the trail by listening to his yelping. When it was treed, we made our way to the spot in the light of our bull's-eye lantern.

The thick glass disk on the globe of the lantern concentrated the rays like a searchlight. One of us would hold the lantern above his head and throw the rays about the naked branches in the hope of finding the coon crouched on a limb. If it looked at the lantern, the reflection of its eyes made it an easy mark for the one with the shotgun. If it failed to give itself away, usually that was the end of the hunting.

If a coon were attacked by a dog on the ground before it could climb a tree, it would put up a stiff fight, sitting on its haunches with its front feet uplifted, turning around in a circle facing the dog, as he attempted to grab it by the nape of the neck. All the time it would be snarling, bristling and showing its sharp teeth and jagged claws. If the dog had the mettle, it could be a life-and-death struggle, but the victory would not always go to the dog.

About the only similarity between the possum and the coon was that both were nocturnal, arboreal animals. The coon had a ringed, bushy tail; the possum a practically hairless, prehensile tail. Their main difference was in their methods of defense. The coon was pugnacious, the possum meek. Instead of fighting in the event of being attacked, it would lie down and pretend to be dead. It would continue to "play possum," irrespective of the nature of the attack. If not too seriously maimed, it would get up and run away after the attack was over. Sometimes it would climb a small tree and hang its prehensile tail over a limb with its head hanging down in full view.

The pelt of a coon would bring about a dollar and that of a possum about one-half as much. Neither a coon nor a possum was considered to be good food, due to the greasy nature of its meat.

The local farmers did not hunt foxes, but sometimes hunters from other localities made their appearance in our neighborhood, riding on horseback. They did not deck themselves in the brilliant colors one sees in some of the old prints. Southwestern Indiana had not reached the state where the people could afford such luxury as English-style dress "to the hounds."

We watched the hunters racing their mounts over the dirt roads and through the open fields, following the hounds in the chase. We heard the barking and yelping of the pack, as they scented the fox. Now and then we saw them as well as reynard as they raced across the fields.

"Sly as a fox" is a well-deserved tribute to this short-legged, point-muzzled, erect-eared and long, bushy-tailed carnivore. It travels in circles, retraces its steps, runs along the tops of logs and fences, jumps off them, takes to water in the ponds and creeks, and performs many other vulpine tricks to throw its pursuers off its track.

Fox hunting was merely a sport, so the hunters themselves never intentionally killed a fox. Although the hounds ran slower, they sometimes were able to overtake it and kill it, due to their greater number. If a fox were captured in a hollow tree or dug out of its lair, it was kept for a chase some later day.

One of the more exciting adventures during my early days was a community bobcat hunt. Someone spread a rumor that a lynx had been seen in the Big Creek Bottoms. The hearsay persisted and the tenseness increased until the farmers decided that an effort should be made to find the predator and exterminate it. Wildcats were carnivorous and farmers were apprehensive that their small domestic animals would be an easy prey.

The woods extended for more than a mile on each side of Big Creek, so the territory to be covered was quite extensive. Several farmers, some with shotguns on their shoulders, some with clubs in their hands, and some with dogs, sallied forth into the Bottoms from each side of Big Creek. The foray took place one dark night in the early winter. The yelping of the dogs added to the commotion, as they ran helter-skelter through the thickets and the woods, sniffing scents along the trails, knowing they were expected to be the star performers.

For a couple of hours, nothing happened of any significance. Then some of the dogs fell onto a hot trail. Soon, the hapless fugitive was brought to bay, took to a tree, and crouched on a limb. When we arrived with our bull's-eye lanterns, the barking of the dogs was at a fever heat and their helpless prey was glaring with its fierce, piercing eyes.

From what we have heard of wildcats, we knew that they were ferocious and savage, especially when cornered on the ground. We felt that if our feline were merely wounded, it would put up a terrific fight on falling out of the tree. Moveover, it might leap down amongst us suddenly and maim some of the men and the dogs. It behooved us to kill it with the first blast in order to be absolutely safe.

Who was the best shot among the posse? The lot fell to our water witch, who often was the winner at the country shooting matches. All of us moved back a safe distance from the tree. He took careful aim with his shotgun, pulled the trigger, and the victim fell to the ground amidst the excited pack. We still kept a safe distance in anticipation of the fray. The woeful captive instantly sprang to its feet and turned round and round on its haunches, snarling and bristling and exposing its sharp teeth and jagged claws, as it fought off the attacks of the howling mob. Before long, the shot began to take effect. Red froth poured from its jaws, choking its angry hisses and growls. Its fierce eyes grew dimmer and dimmer until finally it fell in its own gore.

We approached the tree cautiously to view the result, and what did we find? A wildcat? Nothing but an unusally large coon! I believe the record shows that the last bobcat was seen in Posey County many years prior to the turn of the century.

Environmentalists and naturalists may criticize the hunting events discussed above. Yet hunting was commonplace around the turn of the century and, though mainly done for sport, it lacked the senseless savagery of some other forms of animal persecution, such as trapping.

According to Franklin's Autobiography, he felt that people should abstain from eating fish. Why? Because fish never did people any harm. Later, he learned with surprise that big fish ate little fish. Balancing principle against inclination, he concluded that if the big fish had no qualms against eating the little ones, he should have no scruples against eating the big ones.

Country people had no such compunction. Big Creek was a good place to fish, especially after a good rain. The big fish swam up Big Creek from the Wabash when the water was high and muddy. They included stout-bodied, large-headed catfish and less voracious carp.

We made our own tackle with a cane or a sapling cut for a pole, a cord for a line, a stopper for a float, a piece of lead for a sinker, and a fishhook on which to fasten the worm. This outfit would not have won any prizes for looks but it landed as many fish as any gear bought in a store.

Once, we decided to try our luck in a different way, when the nibbles were few and far between. We flung a stick of dynamite with a lighted fuse into the old swimming hole. The explosion brought to the surface a number of good-sized catfish and carp numbed by the blast. We knew that this kind of fishing was taboo, and that it would have been frowned upon by all fishermen, as well as by our parents. So we gathered up our fish and tackle in a hurry and moved furtively away in order to avoid being caught, and did not repeat it.

Groundhogs were common in Southwestern Indiana. They were of a grizzly gray or reddish-brown color with short stubby tails. They dug their burrows on the hillsides and often under an old stump. They lived in their dens and hibernated during the winter season. Groundhogs destroyed the crops, especially the corn, so we looked upon them as real pests. So much so that now and then we got rid of them with the shotgun and rifle.

According to the folklore, groundhogs ventured out of their burrows on February 2nd to take a look at the weather. If they saw their shadow, they knew that winter would continue for a spell. So they went back into their dens for six weeks more of hibernation. If they failed to see their shadow, they realized that early spring was just around the corner.

Ginseng plants were indigenous to Southwestern Indiana. The plant had a smooth, tender stem several inches long with two to four petioles, each of which had five leaves. We hunted it in the shady places in the woods for its parsnip-like roots, which were used for medicinal purposes. A dry pound sometimes would fetch up to four dollars. Compared to one dollar a day for farmwork, ginseng hunting could be profitable. Today, ginseng roots may sell for several dollars per ounce, depending upon type and locality, though there is no medical proof of the root's pharmacological value.

Country people then never used ginseng for medical purposes or cultivated it for sale. Today, some people "think" it is good for blood pressure, bladder and sinus trouble, nerves and other ailments. According to Department of Agriculture Bulletin No. 2201, several hundred acres are now cultivated annually. It takes about six years for the plant to reach maturity. The price ranges up to $30.00 per pound. About 95 percent of all ginseng grown in the United States, both cultivated and wild, is exported and the balance is used here, chiefly by the Chinese, who believe it has mystical, life-prolonging qualities.

Some country people believed that their blood thickened during the winter and that a spring tonic was needed for its purification. One common remedy was sassafras tea. The aromatic roots of the sassafras tree were cut into small chips and boiled in water until the brew attained a deep, reddish brown like Oriental tea. A cupful in the morning before breakfast was considered to be a proper dosage.

Snipe hunting was a prank, which we sometimes played on our town cousins. The most appropriate time and place was during a dark, moonless night in the woods. We took our dupe into the murky shadows, gave him a gunnysack to hold in his hands, and told him to catch the snipes as we drove them toward him on the ground. After posting him at some gloomy, isolated spot, we went home and left him literally holding the bag. When it finally dawned on him that he had been hoaxed, he groped his way home in the darkness and joined in the fun at his own expense. However, there are many cases of victims becoming terrified and falling prey to psychic ailments after a night alone, lost in the woods.

Shooting matches frequently were held between Thanksgiving and Christmas. Each participant paid a small fee, ten or fifteen cents, for the privilege of shooting. Shotguns were used and all shells contained the same size of shot. The one who came closest to the center of the target won the prize, usually a turkey.

A common custom was called "shooting on the Dutch." It was given this name on account of the large number of Germans living in our neighborhood, "Dutch" being misused for "Deutsch," as in

"Pennsylvania Deutsch." A group of men, carrying shotguns loaded with blank cartridges, gathered at some point on New Year's Eve and walked along the roads and across the fields to a neighbor's house. They sounded off their guns, and the farmer and his wife responded by serving them with cider, apples and cakes.

When a couple married in the country, they were welcomed home with a shivaree, often spelled Chivaree. The neighbors serenaded them with horns, pots, pans, gongs, cowbells and anything else that would make a noise. The newlyweds invited them in and served them refreshments—as if they deserved it!

Around 1900, most country people in the Pocket between the Ohio and the Wabash Rivers had meted out to them what life required but very little more. But a cooperative spirit among them tended to ameliorate the hardships and enable them to enjoy life as well as others on whom Dame Nature beamed a more benignant smile. It might be said with Goldsmith that their best riches were ignorance of wealth and that their best companions were innocence and health. Especially, amongst the youth, a rural mirth uplifted the spirit and dispelled any feeling of dissatisfaction with country life, since they were free of temptations and the vexations of wanting what they could not afford.

CHAPTER TWELVE

New Harmony

AROUND 1900, NEW HARMONY was a village of about 1,300 people. It was known throughout the United States and even abroad for the religious, social, educational and economic theories which were practiced there during the early decades of the nineteenth century.

The hamlet was founded by Father George Rapp, a German pietist preacher and some of his followers. They left their native Germany in 1803 as dissenters to certain doctrines and practices of the Lutheran Church and settled near Pittsburgh, Pennsylvania, in 1805. They established a communal, religious society, which they called Harmonie. Voluntary celibacy was introduced in 1807, due to their belief in the imminent return of Christ and the beginning of the millenium.

The Harmonists, sometimes known as Rappites, believed that their example of harmonious human relations, their communal living, and their peaceful Christian fellowship would induce other communities to adopt a similar policy.

Within about ten years, the Harmonists had outgrown their colony in Pennsylvania. In 1814 and 1815, Rapp and his followers bought more than 20,000 acres of land along the Wabash River in Indiana Territory in what is now Posey County. The site was about ten miles from where my great-grandfather staked his claim in 1815. They sold their property in Pennsylvania and moved lock, stock and barrel to the banks of the Wabash. There they established a new colony which they also called Harmonie. In the course of three or four years, the membership reached about 700.

It should be remembered that when the Rappites made their appearance upon the scene, the southwestern part of Indiana Territory was a wilderness. All of them went to work with a will. They arose between five and six in the morning, had their breakfast, and began their daily work by seven o'clock. They ate three regular meals a day and had mid-morning and mid-afternoon snacks. Curfew rang at nine at night and everyone except the watchman and the shepherds was expected to be indoors. In a few years, a considerable part of the land was cleared and Harmonie became a prosperous community.

Despite the financial success of the venture, the Rappites became disappointed, due chiefly to the difficulties they experienced in shipping their products to distant markets. The only feasible transportation was by way of flatboats on the Wabash, Ohio and Mississippi Rivers. Perhaps another reason was the treatment accorded them by other inhabitants of the county, who looked askance upon their clannishness in speaking German, on their peculiar religious beliefs, and on their communistic theories of property ownership. In 1824, they decided to sell their holdings and to return to Pennsylvania.

The advertisement of the project shows the success that they had achieved during the ten-year period of the colony:

Town of Harmonie with 20,000 acres of first-rate land adjoining, situated on the east bank of the Big Wabash, seventy miles by water from the mouth, only fifteen miles by land from the Ohio River. Wabash is navigable at all seasons for boats of twenty tons burden and a great part of the year for steamboats of middle class. Two thousand acres of highly cultivated land, fifteen of it in vineyard, thirty-five in apple orchard, containing 1,500 bearing apple and pear trees. Considerable peach orchards and pleasure garden with bearing ornamental trees.

One large, three-story water-power merchant mill, extensive factory of cotton and woolen goods, two saw mills, one large brick and stone warehouse, two large granaries, one store, a large tavern, six frame buildings used as mechanics shops, one tanyard of fifty vats, three frame barns 50 x 100 with one threshing machine, three large sheep stables, six two-story brick dwellings 60 x 60, forty two-story brick and frame dwellings, eighty-six log dwellings; all houses have stables and gardens; two large distilleries, one brewery.

In 1825 the Rappites sold their Town of Harmonie, receiving $150,000 for the real estate and $40,000 for their manufactured goods and livestock, and moved back to Pennsylvania. From a financial standpoint, they were unusually successful. When they came to the United States from Germany their average wealth was approximately twenty-five dollars per person. When they sold their holdings on the Wabash, it had increased to around $2,000.*

The purchaser of Harmonie was Robert Owen, a Scottish industrialist, reformer and philanthropist. He had become interested in working conditions of employees generally and had done a great deal to improve the lot of his own at his factory at New Lanark, Scotland.

On February 25, 1825, and again on March 7, 1825, Owen delivered an address in the House of Representatives in Washington before the President of the United States, the Justices of the Supreme Court, Members of the House and the Senate, and other officials of the government on the evils of poverty and class distinctions. He outlined his utopia and what he intended to do to bring it about on the Wabash.

In January, 1826, Owen with a group of some thirty adherents made the trip on a keelboat, *The Philanthropist,* sometimes referred to as the "Boatload of Knowledge," from Pittsburgh down the Ohio to the mouth of the Wabash and up the latter to Harmonie. After his arrival, he made a speech in which he said:

"I am coming to this country to introduce an entirely new state of society, to change it from an ignorant, selfish society to an enlightened social system, which will gradually unite all into one and remove all causes for contests between individuals." His motto was "Universal happiness through universal education."

Owen changed the name of the colony to New Harmony. The

---

*This information is based on Don Blair's *The New Harmony Story* (New Harmony, Indiana: New Harmony Publications Committee), pp. 7–32. It is used with the author's permission.

new society was based on the community ownership of property and equal remuneration for work done, irrespective of its type. There was only one rank; however, preference was given to age and experience.

William Maclure, the principal founder and for more than twenty years the president of the Academy of Natural Sciences at Philadelphia, joined Owen and agreed to finance the schools and the teachers. During the next few years, educators from the eastern part of the United States and from Europe were induced to come to New Harmony.

The principles of the New Utopia set out in its declaration were:

> Equality of rights without regard to sex or other conditions;
> Community ownership of property;
> Freedom of speech and action;
> Courtesy in all intercourse;
> Preservation of health;
> Acquisition of knowledge;
> Obedience to the laws of the country;
> All work to be equal, with everyone on the same footing.*

All persons interested in the new experiment were invited to join at Owen's expense until they were able to support themselves. In a short time, several hundred arrived, representing a heterogeneous collection of devotees, latitudinarians, radicals, lazy theorists and unprincipled sharpers. As a result, dissension soon broke out. The industrious maintained that they were working for the shirkers and the loafers claimed that they were not receiving their share. Trouble also brewed between the professions and the trades, due to everyone's being placed on the same footing. Some of the dissidents seceded and established several communities outside the colony.

Was this a prophetic echo of what was in store for the present generation with its avalanche of "welfare"?

Despite Owen's having taken over a ready-made plant for his experiment, he was bound to fail under such circumstances. He attempted to build an utopian social order in which equal op-

---

*From Blair's *The New Harmony Story,* p. 50. Used with permission.

portunity, cooperative effort and advanced education for all would combine in developing perfect human beings and rid the world of the evils of poverty, competition and exploitation. Human nature was simply not up to the level of his ideals. The dissolution of the society was announced in 1827, and the next year Owen returned to England, where he later became recognized as the founder of British socialism.*

But his experiment in America was not entirely a failure. Those of Owen's followers who remained became leaders in the struggle for free progressive education, abolition of slavery and the emancipation of women from the strictures of the English common law. Maclure and Owen's sons, Robert Dale, David Dale and Richard, and a few others cooperated in developing New Harmony into one of the foremost cultural and educational centers in the United States before the Civil War. It was more famous and more enduring than Brooke Farme at West Roxbury, Massachusetts, the cooperative society of intellectuals and workers during the 1840's, which could boast of Emerson, Dana, Lowell, Parker, Whittier and Greeley as some of its members and sympathizers.

New Harmony became a subject of discussion throughout the United States. European travelers included it in their itinerary. It attracted a number of intellectuals, such as Thomas Say, founder of *American Geology*, Charles Leseur, scientist and antiquarian, and Gerard Troost, a well-known geologist, who settled in New Harmony. Audubon, the famous American ornithologist, visited the village from time to time while he was living at Henderson, Kentucky, some thirty miles away.

New Harmony claims the distinction of being the first place in the United States to have:

> A free public school system
> School for infants
> Kindergarten
> Equal education of the sexes
> Trade school
> Women's literary club with a written constitution

---

*From Blair's *The New Harmony Story*, pp. 32–51. Used with permission.

Free public library
Civic dramatic club
Seat of geological survey
Prohibition of liquor

Some of the first arguments in favor of abolition of slavery were voiced in New Harmony. Frances Wright, who organized the Women's Literary Club, was the first suffragette to advocate the right to vote without regard to sex or color.

One of the unique experiments conducted in New Harmony during the early days was the "time store," operated by Josiah Warren. The store was divided into two parts by a lattice-work. Shelves containing articles for sale were kept in the rear. On the wall at the back of the store in full view of the customer were a clock, a dial, and a board on which were attached the bills paid by the storekeeper to the wholesaler and the prices of the articles for sale.

When the conversation between the storekeeper and the prospective purchaser began, the former set the dial to show when his services began. The buyer was asked if he had a labor note, and if he did not, he was told to obtain one. Labor notes were issued by various individuals indicating the type of services rendered, the number of hours of services to be performed, and the price per hour. If too many labor notes of any particular person were outstanding, they became depreciated. In that event, they either were accepted at a discount or refused altogether. Public opinion was presumed to regulate the value of these notes.

In closing the deal, the buyer gave the storekeeper cash equal to the wholesale price he had paid for the article, plus a small percentage to cover his expenses in operating the store. In addition, the customer gave the storekeeper a labor note equal to the time he had spent in transaction. If the note presented was for a greater amount of time, the storekeeper gave the purchaser a labor note for the difference in time as change.

All of Robert Owen's sons were educated by tutors and in the school of the famous educator, Pestalozzi, at Hofoyl, Switzerland. This may explain in part why New Harmony became so well-known as an educational and cultural center, and why the Owens became so influential in state and national affairs.

Robert Dale Owen was a member of the State Legislature of Indiana from 1836 to 1839. During his incumbency, he was instrumental in having the Legislature enact laws granting married women the right to own and control their own property, the right to their own earnings, the right to inherit one-third of their husband's property in lieu of the common-law right of dower, and making drunkenness a valid ground for divorce. In appreciation of what he had done for them, the women of Indiana placed his statue at one of the entrances of the Capitol Building in Indianapolis.

As a member of the constitutional convention in 1851 and 1852, Robert Dale Owen used his influence to have Indiana adopt the free public school system.*

He was a member of Congress from 1843 to 1848 at the time the question of the acceptance or rejection of the bequest of James Smithson of approximately $600,000.00 to the United States was before the House. There was considerable opposition to accepting a bequest from an Englishman and also to the condition imposed: it was to be used to establish an institution for the increase and diffusion of knowledge among men, and was to be known as the Smithsonian Institution. Owen argued in favor of its acceptance. Following a favorable vote, he introduced the bill in 1845 for the creation of the Smithsonian Institution. It became a law in 1848 and he was one of its first regents.

On September 17, 1862, Robert Dale Owen wrote an eloquent letter to President Lincoln, urging him to issue an emancipation proclamation, which ended with this fervent appeal:

> Lift then the weight from the heart of this people. Let us breathe free once more. Extirpate the blighting curse, a living threat throughout long years past, that has smitten at last with desolation a land to which God has granted everything but wisdom and justice.

---

*This information is based in part on Blair's *The New Harmony Story,* pp. 51-57, and is used with his permission. The description of the "time store" is based on the statement of an unknown writer and appears in Clarence P. Wolfe's *The Story of New Harmony,* pp. 9-10.

Give back to the nation its hopes and faith in a future peace and undisturbed prosperity. Fulfill, you can more than fulfill, the brightest anticipation of those, who in the name of human freedom, and in the face of threats that have ripened into terrible realities since, fought the battle which placed you where you are now.

It is within your power at this very moment not only to consummate an act of enlightened statesmanship, but, as an instrument of the Almighty, to restore freedom to a race of men. If you are tempted by an imperishable name, it is within your reach. We may look through ancient and modern history yet scarce find a sovereign to whom God offered the privilege of bestowing on humanity such a boon so vast.

President Lincoln is reported to have said of the letter: "Its perusal stirred me like a trumpet call."

Secretary Chase wrote Owen a few days before the President signed the Proclamation:

It will be a source of satisfaction to you to know that your letter to the President had more influence on him than any other document which reached him on this subject. I think I may say, more than all others put together. I speak of that which I know from personal conference with him.

It should not surprise anyone that Lincoln and Robert Dale Owen saw eye-to-eye on the slavery question. Both had spent their early years in Southwestern Indiana, where slavery and involuntary servitude were prohibited by the Ordinance of 1787 and later by the Constitution of Indiana in 1816.

David Dale Owen was commissioned by the United States Government to make a geological survey of the lands of the north central states, with headquarters in New Harmony. He later became state geologist of Kentucky, Arkansas and Indiana.

Richard Owen assisted David Dale Owen in the survey of the lands of the northcentral states. He also was a captain in the Mexican War, a lieutenant colonel in the Civil War, professor of geology and chemistry in the Western Military Institute of Kentucky, State Geologist of Indiana, professor of natural sciences at Indiana University, and the first president of Purdue University. His statue stands in the capitol building at Indianapolis, a tribute to him by Confederate prisoners of war and their friends for his humanity while they were under his custodianship during the war.

In 1838, William Maclure founded the Workingman's Institute and Library at New Harmony. He also bequeathed funds to about 160 other libraries, most located in Indiana.

After their flowering, most societies and cultures fade away into a state of quiet desuetude. That was true of New Harmony. By the turn of the century, interest in educational and cultural changes was at a low ebb compared with the grand scale that prevailed there until about 1870. Lockwood's New Harmony Movement, which was studied by the school teachers of Indiana during the early years of the present century, helped to revive the interest in the Rappites and the Owenites and to restore New Harmony to its rightful place among the historic societies today.*

---

*For further studies on New Harmony, see *Encyclopaedia Britannica,* Vol. 16, pp. 305, 980, Vol. 20, p. 837; Robert Dale Owen's *Threading My Way;* Lockwood's *New Harmony Movement;* Holiday's *An Indiana Village;* Nicholson's *The Hoosiers; Dictionary of American Biography* Vol. 14, p. 118; *Indiana Historical Society Publications* Vol. 5, p. 205; Smith's *Early Indiana Trials,* p. 370; Cottman's *Centennial History of Indiana,* p. 93; Thompson's *Stories of Indiana,* p. 155; Don Blair's *The New Harmony Story* and *Harmonist Construction;* Wolfe's *The Story of New Harmony.*

CHAPTER THIRTEEN

Posey County

POSEY COUNTY WAS named after Thomas Posey, the second
Governor of Indiana Territory, who succeeded General William
Henry Harrison in 1812. It was reputed to be the "Hooppole
Township" of Edgar Eggleston's famous frontier novel, *The
Hoosier Schoolmaster.* It has been translated into a number of
foreign languages and is one of the rare books in the Library of
Congress today. The name is supposed to have originated from a
fight between some local coopers and riverboat ruffians at Mt.
Vernon. The barrelmakers routed the riverboatmen by giving them
a good beating with their hooppoles.

William R. Adams, in his Introduction to *Archaeological Notes
on Posey County, Indiana,* 1949, published by the Indiana
Historical Bureau, said:

> Posey County has long been known as an area holding promise of
> great reward for research in prehistory. Through the 120 or so years
> since Charles Alexander Leseur* pioneered in the fields of scientific
> archaeology along the Wabash, many others have added their bit in
> the form of archaeological specimens or reports in print, or both.
> From the county vast quantities 'of artifacts have enriched the
> collections of museums the world over, and private collectors seek-
> ing prizes for their cabinets have found the area a productive
> hunting ground.
>
> This country, as will be noted later, is a transitional zone between
> the north and the south. This fact is reflected in the flora and fauna,

---

*The scientist and antiquarian who settled in New Harmony. See chapter twelve
regarding Leseur.

and likewise in the archaeological materials studied. Perhaps it also may be transitional between the east and the west.

Plants perfectly at home in Georgia, Tennessee, Mississippi and Texas find climate and soil equally agreeable for growth here. Thus the observing visitor to the county will see the American mistletoe adorning the branches of the large trees like "witches broom," where the foliage is off during the winter months. . . . Where cultivation has spared them, the remnants of great cane brakes are to be found, for in early days the southern cane was a prominent and irritating feature of Posey County vegetation. The southern cypress was once a common tree but now due to unjudicious cutting it is almost a thing of the past. Fortunately, a large stand has been preserved by the State of Indiana and here at Hovey's Lake the visitor can visualize in part at least how much of the southwestern bottom lands of Indiana once looked.

On many bottom land farms today one will see one or more large elm-shaped trees which have been spared, even though standing in cultivated fields. These are pecan trees, which have some economic importance even today as they did many years ago for the original inhabitants.

Southwestern Indiana, and Posey County in particular, contains evidence of intensive occupation by aboriginal groups over a long period of time. The earliest occupants may have been people of the late Folsom* times, if we can accept the discovery of a good example of a fluted point as such evidence.

At least twelve principal mounds were discovered not far from the Ohio and Wabash rivers, one about 1,500 feet long and 150 feet wide. By 1900 some of them had been eroded and washed away by the flood waters of the rivers.

Human and animal skeletons, ceramics, clay figurines, pipes, bottles, effigy bowls, copper beads, headdresses, discs, ear coils, helmets and buttons, stamped pendants, celts, sherds, shell ornaments, chisels, arrowheads, abrading sandstones, flint-flaked knives, hammers and anvils have been exhumed from these prehistoric graves.

Mt. Vernon, the county seat, was settled in 1805. By 1817 it still had only seventeen families; but around 1900 it was a good example

---

*A prehistoric culture on the east side of the Rocky Mountains. Characterized by flint projectile points having a concave base with side projections and a longitudinal groove on each face.

This excerpt reprinted with permission of the Indiana Historical Bureau.

of a quiet residence town of about 5,000 people, with wide streets lined with elms, maples and poplars, and with modest, comfortable homes.

Short stretches of the roads radiating from town were covered with gravel, but beyond they were mere dirt. The most famous road in the county was the plank road, which was constructed about the middle of the century between New Harmony and Mt. Vernon. It occupied only one side of the road and was made of boards ten feet long, twelve to eighteen inches wide and three inches thick, laid perpendicularly to the road. Toll posts lined the road one mile apart, and three cents a mile was collected for its use. Drivers with light loads were required to turn off the planks on to the dirt side, when they met someone with a heavier load. The maintenance of this road was so expensive that it was abandoned shortly after the Civil War. It has continued to be called the Old Plank Road.

A covered bridge over Big Creek at Solitude on the Old Plank Road a few miles north of Mt. Vernon was still in use around 1900. A few other covered bridges were located in different parts of the county at that time. They had heavy timber frames, plank floors, board sides and clapboard roofs. On rainy days they sometimes were a refuge for travellers during downpours and storms; and at night they were reputed to be hangouts for ghosts. Now and then a tramp made one of them his sleeping quarters for the night; and occasionally a highwayman lay in wait and robbed an unwary traveller in the darkness. One had an eerie feeling on driving through an old covered bridge in the pitch-black darkness and hearing the noise of the horses' feet trampling and the sound of the iron tires of his buggy or wagon treading over the plank floor and reverberating from the roof and the board sides.*

The officials of the county—the judge, clerk, sheriff, assessor, recorder, auditor, treasurer and superintendent of the schools—had their offices in the 120-feet-tall brick courthouse. It was built in

---

*See Anne E. Kelly's *The Plank Road* (1951), a pamphlet available at the Library of Congress, for discussion of the plank road between Mt. Vernon and New Harmony. Notes on this road are also available at the Maclure Workingman's Institute and Library in New Harmony.

1875 on a slightly elevated square in the center of Mt. Vernon at a cost of $95,000.00. It followed the pattern of the State Capitol at Indianapolis in having a towering dome. The courthouse over-shadowed the two-story buildings on the side streets and was very impressive, especially to people who lived in the country.

The farmers and their families usually went to town on Saturday afternoons. One could hear the jingling of the trace chains, the creaking of the harnesses, the tramping of the horses' feet and the grinding of the metal tires of the buggies and wagons over the gravelly streets as they drove in. After tethering their horses to the hitching posts, the country folk proceeded to sell their produce, buy groceries and wares, attend to official business in the court-house and talk over legal matters with their lawyers.

A half-dozen lawyers had their shingles out on Fourth Street north of the courthouse square. At that time, it was not necessary for a lawyer to be a graduate of law school or to have read law under the supervision of a practicing attorney. The Constitution of Indiana guaranteed to every voter of good moral character the right to practice law. Most of the Posey County lawyers were skillful advocates.

A lawyer had one or two rooms, which usually contained a rolltop desk, revolving chair, two or three straight-backed chairs, small iron safe, and the Indiana Statutes and the Reports of the Appellate and Supreme Courts of the state. Trials were held in the courtroom of the Posey Circuit Court, on the second floor of the courthouse.

The early judges rode the circuit and held court in various places. They and the accompanying lawyers usually travelled on horseback and stayed in cheap boarding-houses or hotels. This called for a rugged constitution on the part of the bench as well as the bar.

According to Leonard's *History of Posey County* the rulings of one of the early judges were so contrary to the law and his tem-perament was so unjudicial, that the bar succeeded in having him removed and another judge appointed in his place. This caused him to be very resentful toward his successor. Once, while he was acting as counsel, he disputed the ruling of the new judge with such animosity and insolence that the judge ruled him to show cause why he should not be held in contempt of court. At that he became so outraged that the other lawyers were apprehensive that he might attack the judge. When the case came up for hearing, one of them slipped a dagger wrapped in a handkerchief to the judge on the bench, for self-protection. Sure enough, the attack was attempted; but the judge was able to ward off the blows with the dagger until someone grabbed the assailant from behind. A fine of $50.00 and ten days in jail were imposed upon the obstreperous advocate, who retaliated by suing the judge for false imprisonment. He soon recanted and dismissed the suit.

Now and then, a murder was committed in the county, and the accused was tried in Mt. Vernon. People from all over the county flocked to court to witness the proceedings, for a court trial provided the only real drama at that time. Movies and theaters had not made their way into Mt. Vernon.

One brutal murder was committed in the county, which never reached the court. A sadist habitually tortured his wife by nailing the window down over her fingers and forcing her to stay in that position until he condescended to release her. Finally, he killed her in cold blood, and the people were up in arms. He was arrested in Evansville and lodged in jail there. A mob assembled in Posey County, intent upon breaking into the jail and lynching him in his own home by setting it on fire. They succeeded in breaking into jail and kidnapping the murderer, but the Evansville police intervened and dispersed the mob; however, not before one of them had dispatched the prisoner by hitting him on the head with a hammer. None of the mob was ever tried for participating in lynch-law justice.

A case which elicited considerable interest arose in Oliver Station. As the owner of the village store was going home one night, a man accosted him in the darkness and yelled, "I have got you now!" The storekeeper backed away, hoping to avoid the encounter. His assailant put his hand in his pocket, indicating that he intended to carry out his threat. He was too slow, though, as his intended victim was quicker on the draw and shot him with his pistol.

The storekeeper was indicted for manslaughter and tried before a jury in Mt. Vernon. He was defended by the Nestor of the bar, famous for his legal victories at home and abroad. Counsel was adept in forensics and well versed in the Scriptures. He took for his text the passage in Deuteronomy, "but if any man hate his neighbour, and lie in wait for him, and rise up against him, and smite him mortally that he die . . ." (Deut. 19:11). Following an impassioned plea, interspersed with frequent references to the Bible and terse aphorisms, the jury found the defendant not guilty.

In a later case, though, he was found guilty of carrying a concealed weapon and given a fine. Apparently the authorities felt that a minor misdemeanor should not be waived even when a person was defending his own life.

A case in a more humorous vein involved mayhem. Two men engaged in a fight in which one of them lost a piece of his ear. The other was indicted for biting it off. After both of the participants had testified, the result did not look very promising for the defendant. He felt that he might improve his position by calling John Doe as a witness, who was at the scene of the fighting and saw everything. The witness took the stand on direct examination:

"Mr. Doe, do you know the defendant and were you present at the fight?"

"Sure I was."

"Well, tell us just what you saw."

"I was coming along the road and I seen them getting up out of the dirt; but I didn't see anybody hit anybody; and I didn't see anybody kick anybody; and I didn't see anybody bite off anybody's ear."

"You were in plain view and you didn't see any of these things happen?"

"I didn't see any of these things at all."

Then the prosecutor took over.

"Now, Mr. Doe, you have told us everything which you *didn't* see. Suppose you just tell what you *did* see."

"Well, it is so, I didn't see anybody hit anybody; and I didn't see anybody kick anybody; and I didn't see anybody bite off anybody's ear; but just as I got up to where they were fighting, I saw the defendant spit a piece of somebody's ear out of his mouth."

"So you saw the defendant spit a piece of the plaintiff's ear out of his mouth?"

"No. I didn't try to see whether it would fit."

The courtroom naturally responded to that seriocomic routine with much laughter.

A justice of the peace was elected in each of the ten townships of the county. He had jurisdiction of cases in contract and tort up to $100.00. A woman sued another woman in a justice of the peace's court for slander, claiming damages of $50.00 to her reputation. The basis of the suit was that the defendant had accused the plaintiff of stealing her gander. The plaintiff first testified that she was the owner; then she called a dignified old lady, who testified that the gander belonged to the plaintiff. The defendant's lawyer cross-examined her as follows:

"How do you know that this particular gander belongs to the plaintiff?"

"I owned the grandfather of plaintiff's gander, and he paced. I also owned the father of plaintiff's gander, and he paced. I know that this is plaintiff's gander, because he paces just like his father and his grandfather."

Judgment was entered for plaintiff; but it might have been different if the defendant's lawyer had known that all ganders pace.

While the cases before justices of the peace were few and usually simple, none compared in pettiness with a legendary case in ancient Greece. There, a man hired his ass to his neighbor. One hot summer day, he came upon his neighbor lying on the ground in the shade of his ass. The owner protested vigorously and later brought suit for additional rent. The theory was that the letting of his ass did not carry with it the use of its shadow.*

---

*From Apuleius' Latin work, "The Golden Ass," circa 180 A.D.

All county officers were elected by the voters. During the campaigns the candidates travelled about the county selling themselves to the farmers and village residents. Most of the lawyers got into politics in one way or another. They were accustomed to public speaking, and either campaigned for someone else or ran for county judge themselves.

Two lawyers of my acquaintance were partners. Apparently, they did not confide in each other completely, for one of them was nominated for county judge on the Republican ticket. When he told his partner, the latter informed him that he too was to be nominated for judge—on the Democratic ticket. They fought it out in the campaign. The Republican won, leaving his Democratic partner to carry on the practice.

Mt. Vernon was the scene of political rallies during presidential and congressional campaigns. My earliest recollection of such an event was in 1896, when William Jennings Bryan was a candidate for the presidency for the first time. He had become famous overnight due to his Cross of Gold speech in the Democratic convention in Chicago that summer. Tom took me to the rally. An old-fashioned torchlight parade accompanied with bands took place along Main Street, which was lined with people from all over the county. After the pomp and ceremony were over, the crowd gathered in the courtroom to hear Bryan's speech. He made a very flowery and impassioned address, for which he was to become famous in later years. He condemned the trusts, the protective tariff, the gold standard, and other planks of the Republican Party, and advocated free trade and the unlimited coinage of silver at the ration of sixteen-to-one. It was my privilege to see him stampede the Democratic Convention in Baltimore sixteen years later in favor of the nomination of Woodrow Wilson for the presidency.

Democrats and Republicans vied with one another in putting on the biggest, noisiest, brightest and liveliest show. When the Democrats held a parade, their houses along the street were gayly lighted and decorated, inside and out; but the homes of the Republicans were dark. When the Republicans' turn came, their houses were brilliantly illuminated and embellished; but the homes of the Democrats were black as night. Each party hired extra marchers to prove that its party was the people's choice.

CHAPTER FOURTEEN

Lincoln's Indiana Home

IN THE FALL OF 1816, Thomas Lincoln made a scouting trip from his home in Kentucky into Southwestern Indiana in search of a new home. He selected a tract of 160 acres near Little Pigeon Creek in what is now Spencer County. It was about fifteen miles north of the Ohio River and forty miles east of where my great-grandfather staked his claim in 1815. He piled brush and notched trees at the four corners of his claim to comply with the law requiring the staking of claims on public lands. He then returned to Kentucky to settle his affairs and to make preparations for taking his family to their new Indiana home.

Early in the following December, his wife, Nancy Hanks, his nine-year-old daughter, Sarah, his seven-year-old son, Abraham, and he gathered their meager clothing, bedding, cooking utensils, rifle, tools and Bible and began their 100-mile journey.

On the third day they reached the Ohio River and crossed it in a ferry boat at Thompson's Ferry near what is now Rockport. They trekked the remaining fifteen miles in an ox-drawn wagon with wheels crosscut from logs. They borrowed the wagon and the oxen from Francis Posey, a settler on the Indiana side of the Ohio. The first twelve miles of the trek were along an existing wagon trail. For the remaining three miles, it was necessary to hack a trace through the practically impenetrable forest. They finally reached their claim in mid-December, 1816, without a horse, cow, wagon or house of their own.

The weather was bitter cold. The first necessity was a shelter, which probably was a windowless lean-to-camp. The shanty was built between two trees fourteen feet apart. Three of the sides were made of unhewn logs piled on top of one another, with mud, grass and leaves filling the cracks. The south side was open, but probably protected to some extent with skins covering the breach. The roof also was made of poles, brush and leaves. The floor was the bare ground with leaves strewn over it. Bunches of leaves packed on the floor were used as beds. A log fireplace near the open side of the camp performed the triple function of furnishing illumination during the nighttime, heat to warm the camp, and fire to cook the meals.

This temporary lean-to was the shelter of the Lincoln family for only a short time. For life was miserable enough when the weather was clear and cold; it became almost insufferable when the blustery wind blew the rain and snow through the open end and filled the shack with smoke from the log-burning fire.

Early in 1817, a one-room, floorless, windowless, eighteen-foot-square log cabin was completed to take the place of the temporary shelter. A stick chimney plastered with clay ran up the outside wall to carry away the smoke of the log fire. The beds were made of boards ripsawed from logs and poles cleated into the corners of the room. The bedding consisted of blankets brought from Kentucky, skins obtained from wild animals in the nearby woods, and leaves gathered from the trees. The cabin had a sleeping loft, which was reached by climbing up a makeshift ladder of pegs driven into the side of the wall.

Water was carried in buckets by Sarah and Abraham from a spring about a mile away.

The Lincoln cabin was located about a mile from a country store owned by a settler known as James Gentry, for whom the settlement of Gentryville was named.

A small patch of woods was cleared and planted to corn, which in time was increased to about forty acres. Meal was made by pestling grains of corn in a stump hollowed out in the shape of a mortar. The forest supplied an abundance of turkeys, partridges, grouse, ducks, geese, rabbits, deer, nuts, grapes and other wild fruits. In due time, the Lincolns acquired a few sheep, cattle and hogs, and a horse.

During the fall of 1817, relatives of Nancy Hanks arrived from Kentucky—Thomas and Elizabeth Sparrow, her uncle and aunt, and Dennis Hanks, the Sparrows' eighteen-year-old nephew.

The winter of 1817 and 1818 was severe. The nearest doctor lived thirty miles away, and the roads were mere strips cut through the woods. Several of the settlers were carried away with the milk fever, including the Sparrows and Nancy Hanks. Thomas Lincoln buried them in boxes, which he made of boards ripsawed from logs and fastened together with wooden pegs, on a knoll on his farm about a quarter-mile from his cabin.

The fever which carried away the early settlers was known as milk fever, because it was believed to have come from drinking milk. Years later, medical authorities decided that it did come from drinking the milk of cows that had eaten a poisonous plant known as snakeroot.

A log church and a log schoolhouse were built by the community. Abraham and Sarah walked to school, which was at least a mile away. This lasted for only a few months and was the only formal schooling Abraham ever received, except for a short period in Kentucky before the family moved to Indiana. He himself said that he got his schooling by "littles," which probably was less than one year altogether. Despite this handicap, he was more interested in books than in chopping down trees, or splitting rails, or plowing corn. He borrowed all the books he could put his hands on in Boonville and Rockport, and he lay on the floor before the fireplace fire, poring over them. One of his biographers stated that he longed to go to school at New Harmony on the Wabash, as he watched the pack horses and oxteams passing through Gentryville and headed in that direction.

Abraham's first glimpse of a somewhat wider view of the world may have come to him when he worked on a farm near the Ohio River and operated a ferry from the Indiana side to the middle of the river for six dollars a month, and later when he made a trip down the Ohio and Mississippi to New Orleans for James Gentry, for eight dollars a month. This trip brought him into contact with slavery at first-hand and had a tremendous influence on him in later life.

In 1829 Abraham and his father built another log house which, however, they never occupied. Around 1874 it was shipped to Rockport and taken on barges to Cincinnati, where it was converted into relics and souvenirs of the President's early beginnings.

The Lincoln days in Indiana ended in 1830, when Thomas Lincoln contracted the pioneer fever again and moved what was left of his family to Illinois.

The 1817 log cabin in which the Lincoln family lived for fourteen years disappeared before the turn of the century. It is doubtful whether any evidence existed around 1900 that the Lincolns had ever lived near Gentryville, except the graves of Nancy Hanks and Sarah, and the small patch of ground they cleared. The unmarked shrine was not forgotten; but very few people made the pilgrimage from Posey County. A round trip of 100 miles by horseback or by horse and buggy over unpaved roads most of the way was a hardship which no one within my acquaintance was willing to incur. The homage due Abraham Lincoln did not manifest itself at Gentryville until later years.

Abraham Lincoln's Indiana home was about forty miles from Posey County. It was established at practically the same time as my great-grandfather built his home and the Rappites began to build New Harmony.

CHAPTER FIFTEEN

Sentimental Journey

WHEN ONE PLANS to make a pilgrimage to the scenes of his youth, not the least of his concerns should be the time of year most favorable for the visit. It seemed to me that early May would be the ideal season, when the dogwoods and redbuds would be adorning the woodlands, the apple, peach, plum and pear trees embellishing the orchards, and the spring flowers decorating the fencerows, the roadsides, and the fringes of the woods. The weather too should be suitable for hiking over the old farm and for visiting venerable neighbors who must surely be round-about. In the past no one moved except for good reason, and many of them must have continued to love the land as I did.

Another concern should be the way to make the journey. At the turn of the century, the only alternative to travelling between Washington and Southwestern Indiana by horseback, or by buggy or wagon over unimproved roads, at least for a part of the way, was by railroad train. My trip could have been made via Pittsburgh, Indianapolis and Terre Haute, or by way of Charleston, Cincinnati and Vincennes. Despite the greater comfort and speed by air, I decided to make the trip to the old home-place by train over the northern route. There was a tinge of nostalgia in this decision, as I had taken this route a number of times while attending law school at the George Washington University in Washington many years ago.

As the train approached Indianapolis, recollections of the Officers' Training Camp at nearby Fort Benjamin Harrison flashed through my mind—the drilling, marching, parading, digging trenches and studying military tactics during the daytime, and attending lectures at night. And at the end of three months' training the transformation of amateur civilians into military officers to serve in the First World War.

The stopover at Terre Haute offered an opportunity to visit the Indiana State University, known as the Indiana State Normal School at the time of my attendance. The new university bears no resemblance to the old normal school—thirty buildings, 10,000 students, and tuition of several hundred dollars per semester today, compared with two buildings, a few score students, and a library fee of only two dollars a term at the turn of the century.

Upon my arrival at Evansville, an automobile was awaiting me. Soon, the last lap of the journey was under way, starting over the Evansville-New Harmony Turnpike. This was the last leg of the trip we used to take to Evansville from the farm. Instead of the rough, gravelly road I knew, it is a smooth, two-lane concrete highway today.

The first familiar sight was the mill on Bunker Hill, where we used to leave a bag of wheat and corn on the way into town and to pick up the grist on the way home.

It seemed natural to turn to the left on the old wagon road, at Parkers Settlement, which should take me to the old homestead.

Give me the country road for a quiet, leisurely ride up hill and down dale, and let others repine at the lack of turnpike thoroughfares. One is able to enjoy the scenery of the countryside along the way without keeping one's eyes glued to the road to avoid being run down by a reckless driver.

The old wagon road has been improved somewhat since the early days, with a covering of loose gravel, but it is as narrow as ever, just wide enough for two cars to pass by going slowly and edging over to the sides of the road.

So many new houses lined the way, and the contour of the road itself seemed to be so different from what I recalled, that I began to doubt whether it was the old wagon road, after all.

I stopped and asked a farmer on a tractor in a nearby field, "Will this road take me to the Old Downen School House?"

"Never heard of it. Where is it?"

"On this side of Big Creek, about three miles this side of Oliver."

"I think you are on the right road. When you reach two or three houses in a clump of trees at the top of a hill about three miles from here, turn left, and then take the next turn to the right."

Thanking him and driving on, I was preoccupied with ruminations. Would the old house and barn look the same? Would the bluegrass pasture across the road be as green as it used to be? Would the two springs down the valley be giving forth their clear, cold waters as they did of yore? Would the murmuring brook be singing its lilting melody? Would the little ripples be swerving around the pebbles and joining hands on their way to Big Creek? Would the willow trees be quivering in the sunlight?

Thus prepossessed by memory and expectation, I bypassed the right turn beyond the houses at the top of the hill and continued a couple of miles, before realizing my mistake. After backtracking to the junction of the roads and going another mile, finally the old farm came into view.

And what an unfamiliar sight!

CHAPTER SIXTEEN

The Deserted Homestead

THE OLD HOMESTEAD had been abandoned for farming some forty years ago. Soon after they were forsaken, the frame house and barn were razed by fire. Everything—the driveway, garden, orchard, barnyard, blue grass pasture and fields—was overgrown with a wilderness of vines, briars, underbrush, sprouts, saplings and trees. Some of the trees, none of which had even been seedlings when I lived there, were forty feet tall. White oaks, yellow poplars, ashes, dogwoods, sycamores, locusts, black walnuts, sweetgums, maples and sassafrases all had been invading the old farm ever since it was deserted. Nature had been exercising her sovereign right of restoring the forest, which we devastated around the turn of the century, and of reclaiming the entire farm as her own. But in this case, Nature's gain was my loss.

It was barely possible to drive the car off the narrow road into the old driveway, so dense and tangled was the undergrowth. With considerable effort I stepped about the yard where the old house used to be. The only recognizable landmarks were the dilapidated cistern, the collapsed well, the caved-in cellar and the venerable maple tree near the edge of the road. The kaleidoscopic view of the western horizon that we used to enjoy was now blotted out by the thick growth of saplings and trees.

After surveying the situation for several minutes, and with a sinking heart, it became clear that it would be extremely difficult for me to walk about the old farm. Even if I were able to penetrate the thicket, my vision would be restricted to only a few feet. Under these circumstances, it seemed futile to attempt to ferret out any old haunts of bygone days.

I drove the car down the hill between the encroaching copse on each side of the road in the direction of Big Creek. Another landmark stood out conspicuously in the midst of the saplings and trees—the old elm tree, now apparently dead, in which the mourning doves used to sit and emit their plaintive coos and prognosticate the coming rain.

Farther down the road, I met a local resident and introduced myself.

"I used to live in a frame house at the top of the hill near the junction of the roads."

"I do not remember your name nor recollect ever seeing the house," he said.

"That is not surprising, as the time was so long ago."

When I mentioned the name of another farmer, who lived nearby many years ago, he said that he never had heard of him, either.

"Did you ever hear of the Downen School?"

"Yes, but it was torn down years ago."

"I am on my way to Oliver Station and intend to continue through the Big Creek Bottoms over the old road I used to travel about seventy years ago."

"You will have to give up that idea. There is no such road any more. You would be lucky even to walk along the old trail, where the road used to be. You couldn't possibly get through with an automobile. The road is as overgrown as your old farm."

"That seems incredible," I said, feeling that surely some citizens would have cared enough about it to see that it was kept passable.

"But it is true. The only way you can get to Oliver is over the other road a couple of miles to the south."

Disheartened by the news, I strolled down the hill the remaining three or four hundred yards to the Creek. The bridge was indeed in a high state of deterioration. The bottoms and the banks of Big Creek were covered with willows, bushes and saplings. The water was a narrow, shallow skein of yellow, its bed littered with dead limbs and logs. The channel was being filled with mud. It was apparent that the floodwaters from heavy rains would cover the bottoms several feet deep and recede very slowly, under such conditions.

Before starting on my pilgrimage, it had been my hope to walk down the valley across the old bluegrass pasture and commune with the twin springs that used to gush forth their clear, sparkling water, year after year. Watching cold, crystal spring water issuing from the side of a hill or a mountain has always been a fascination to me, marvelling whence it comes, whither it goes, and how long ago it began. I have sat at the foot of Mt. Parnassus at Delphi and been captivated by the waters of the Castalia Spring gushing and bubbling and gurgling from the side of the mountain as they have been doing for thousands of years. Were the twin springs in the old bluegrass pasture still flowing as they did sixty or seventy years ago?

It seemed astonishing that a bluegrass pasture could become an impenetrable thicket in only a few decades. I decided to make a reconnaisance to find some way, if possible, to penetrate the coppice. After a careful survey, the south side of the pasture seemed to offer the least resistance.

With the help of a post, I clambered over the wire fence, trod slowly along the side of the slope, stepped gingerly over dead limbs, through vines and briars, wended my way through thick underbrush, saplings and trees, leaped over ditches—and finally reached my goal.

Many times, years ago, I had lain prone on the ground and slaked my thirst with the pure cold water flowing from these twin springs. If I had known before commencing my pilgrimage what would actually confront me, it is doubtful whether I would have made the trip. No clear, sparkling, bubbling water issued from the hillsides; no gurgling water trickled down the rill, its murmur inviting indolent repose as of old. Only stagnant water oozed through a maze of vines, brush, humus, leaves and other debris, moving sluggishly down the forlorn, littered brook. With so many impediments obstructing the flow, it seemed doubtful whether any of the seepage ever found its way to Big Creek about a mile away.

After standing there for several minutes in a mood of nostalgia, recalling the marvellous contribution which these two springs once had made to man and beast, not to say to my own memories, I plodded back up the hill considerably slower than in going down. With a feebleness in my arms and legs and a dampness in my spirits, I laboriously pulled myself over the wire fence on to the road.

I stood there in sad reverie for a long while. It was one of those moments when memory asserts its magical power over the present and illuminates the vistas of retrospection with an effulgence far greater than during ordinary times. For many years, our family had labored, clearing the forest, sowing the seed, harvesting the grain. True, we started out moderately poor and never accumulated many of the material things of this life. But this had been our home, which had sheltered us in all kinds of weather for many a year.

All of our work had come to naught. Look where I would, there was not the slightest evidence that the old farm ever had been touched with a plow.

In retrospect, our father stood before me, a man who had worked hard for his family and had taught us self-reliance in the true Emersonian vein. He was a disciplinarian who tempered his training with justice. Perhaps it was fortunate that he did not see the result of his toil.

I resolved to learn, if possible, how a farm could revert to Nature in such a short time without the intervention of man. On my return to Washington, an official in the government satisfied my curiosity.

"How is it possible for a forest to grow on an abandoned farm without the help of man?" I asked.

"It comes about by the dissemination of the seeds of trees from the nearby woods."

"In what way?"

"The winds blow the light seeds, such as those of the pines, spruces, yellow poplars, ashes, maples, birches, sycamores and elms. These seeds are attached to wings and other light, downy materials. The wind then carries them away from the parent trees. Birds eat seed-bearing fruit, like blackberries and raspberries. In due course, they drop these seeds here and there away from their place of growth. Jays and other birds are known to carry acorns and pecans, hide them under leaves or on the ground, and then forget where they hid them. Squirrels and other rodents carry heavy seeds, such as acorns, walnuts, hickory nuts and pecans away from their parent trees and bury them in the ground. These various seeds take hold and begin to grow."

"About what is the order of the new growth?"

"Take your abandoned farm. The summer after cultivation stopped, tall weeds began to grow in the fields from the seeds already there and those dropped by birds. Bunches of grass began to grow among the weeds, the first and second seasons. Raspberry and blackberry seeds started to take root. The new growth dropped their seeds and this continued year after year, until the land was smothered by underbrush and sprouts. At the end of five years, your farm was already a tangle of briars, grasses and clumps of underbrush and sprouts. The sprouts grew into saplings and in ten years your old farm was a young forest, higher than your head. In twenty years the hardwoods and softwoods had made considerable inroads, and in forty years you would never believe that your home place had ever been plowed."

"What are the best conditions for a new forest on old land?"

"Good ground, air, rain and sunshine make the best forest. Climate is one of the main factors. Another is the proximity of the new forest to its ancestors, which already have become acclimated to the soil and weather conditions. If left alone, a forest perpetuates itself. Before many years, the skunks, possums, coons, minks, rabbits and squirrels begin to make it their habitation. I am sure you would find some of them now, if you were to invade their domain on your old farm."

"How long is it before trees reach the sawlog stage?"

"Hardwood trees require 100 to 120 years. Softwoods take up to seventy years. For the best sawlogs, it would be necessary to double the time.''

"Quite a number of hill farms have been abandoned in Indiana. What is the reason for this situation?'' I asked, realizing that my own situation might not be as atypical as I had imagined.

"Hilly land never was economical for farming. When farms began to be mechanized with tractors and combines, the cost became prohibitive and hill farmers had to throw in the sponge.''

After coming out of my reverie, and realizing more than ever that the only thing that remains the same is change, I motored down the old dirt road, covered with loose gravel, to the ancient graveyard, skirted it along the north side and continued over the serpentine lane to the site of Grandmother's venerable log house.

It, too, had disappeared. My mind turned back to those cold, wintry winds that raged around the old log house, penetrating the cracks around the windows and doors and sucking the fireplace blazes up the chimney with a swish into the darkness of night. Gone, too, was the log barn at the bottom of the lane, where the horses and cows used to wait for us at feeding time.

The graveyard also is on the way to obliteration. Some of the tombstones had fallen and were lying on their sides. But then, I thought, why should one expect otherwise? Where are the graves of Socrates and Pericles of classical Greece and the final resting places of the Caesars of ancient Rome?

No sign of the one-room, red brick schoolhouse on the south side of the graveyard. More surprisingly, not a single maple tree that we planted around the turn of the century was standing sentinel over the site. The schoolyard was being used for the growing of corn. At least something, I thought ruefully, is being put to good use.

The old lane that formerly ran past the schoolyard and joined the south road to Oliver was unrecognizable, except where slight evidence of the wagon tracks remained.

I continued to Oliver alongside the strip of woods we used to hunt for wild grapes in the fall and early winter. The flowers were swaying and the leaves were rustling gently, as I had remembered; they were being stroked the wrong way by the breeze. Meadowlarks still flitted from bough to bough and sang in the open spaces. Turtle doves were fluttering, cooing, alighting in couples beside the road. Bobwhites were preempting the way in front, as coveys crossed over in single file. Occasionally, a rabbit nibbled clover or scampered along the road. At least, there was no change in bird or animal life, I thought wistfully—and perhaps that was just as it should be.

CHAPTER SEVENTEEN

Gone the Horse and Buggy Days

THE COUNTRY DOCTOR and barber, like the dance hall and saloon, have all passed from the scene in Oliver Station like chaff blown away by the wind. Somewhat reassuringly, the old blacksmith shop still stands at the same spot, although there are no more horses to be shod, no more redhot steel plowshares to be hammered on the anvil, no more cast-iron plowshares to be sharpened on the foot-treadle emery wheel. Today's smithy uses an electric welder instead of the old, hand-operated flaming forge to repair farm implements unknown when I was growing up on the farm.

During the 1950s, a natural gas field, known as the Oliver Pool, was discovered near the village. The reservoir is used to store natural gas piped from Louisiana and Texas, to provide a supply for Evansville and other towns and villages in Southwestern Indiana during the peak winter season. Oil, too, has been discovered in paying quantities near Oliver and in various other places in the county, and its equipment has added to the changes in the land.

The most noticeable change in the county, though, has been the revolution in agriculture. Some of the best farmland in the United States is located in the pocket between the Ohio and the Wabash rivers. The soil is very fertile and comparatively level due to the alluvial deposits of floodwaters, making much of the land superbly adaptable to mechanization. As a consquence, draft animals, buggies, wagons, walking and riding plows, A-type harrows, one-row corn planters and two-shovel cultivators, shucking pegs, horse-drawn reapers and steam-powered threshing machines have been superseded by tractors, automobiles, trucks, multiple mouldboard plows, corn planters and cultivators, wide-disc harrows, wheat and corn combines and other modern machines.

The tractor, of course, is the keystone of the latest revolution in agriculture. The transformation has been more important than the epochal change that began in the 1830s with the introduction of the steel mouldboard plow, the wheat and corn drills, the horse-drawn reaper, the threshing machine and the steam engine, which shifted from the backs of the farmers the burden of the ages to animal and steam power. It was between 1915 and 1920 that the tractor first came into practical and widespread use on the farm. The First World War gave it a considerable boost, due to the necessity of releasing farmers for the armed forces and of increasing the food supply for our allies and ourselves. With the advent of the tricycle-type tractor in 1923 and the substitution of rubber for steel tires in 1932, which increased the power and the speed about one-fourth and saved up to one-fifth of the fuel, the gasoline-burning tractor was well on its way to replacing all power, human, animal and steam, that had been used in farming prior to that time.

The tractor eliminated draft animals for farming, decreased the number of farmers needed to grow the necessary food, and increased the acreage available for its production. When it made its first appearance, some 26,500,000 draft animals were in use in the United States and thirty percent of the people were engaged in farming. Today, there are only approximately 3,000,000 horses. Most are saddle-horses, and very few are draft animals. The percentage of the population engaged in agriculture has dwindled to less than five percent.

During the draft-animal power age, five acres of land were required to grow the feed needed for a single animal. Today, the time of the farmer and the millions of acres released from growing feed are available for the production of food not only for the people of the United States but also for foreign nations.

The one-bottom walking and riding plows have been replaced by multiple-bottom mouldboard plows capable of turning furrows sixteen to eighteen inches wide and twelve to fourteen inches deep. With a large plow and a tractor, one man is able to plow up to fifty acres of land in a single day, compared with one or two acres with a one-bottom plow seventy years ago.

Instead of the one-row corn planter and the double-shovel plow to cultivate the corn, the farmer today uses multiple-row planters and cultivators. The conventional method is to plow and then disc the ground before planting, although the discing sometimes is dispensed with. This is especially true where a soil pulverizer is attached to the front of the planter and breaks up the soil simultaneously with the planting. As the corn seeds are dropped, an insecticide now falls in the rows to do away with the worms, a pre-emergence herbicide is sprayed on each side of the rows to kill the weeds and grass, and a fertilizer is applied to maintain the soil.

Combines, with air-conditioned cabins in which the farmers ride, come equipped with telephone and radio. They pick four or more rows of corn and shell it in one operation, while the driver listens to his favorite country music! The best farmland produces up to 200 bushels of corn to the acre, where the most scientific methods are utilized. One large combine can pick and shell from 4,000 to 5,000 bushels of corn in one day, compared with sixty to seventy bushels husked with the old hand-shucking peg.

The ground is plowed and disced, or sometimes only disced, with harrows up to fourteen feet wide before sowing wheat. Sometimes, two or three disc harrows are latched laterally and the ground harrowed is increased accordingly. The method of sowing wheat has not changed materially since the turn of the century, but the drill is wider and the drop hoes have been replaced by discs to implant the seed. A combine is used to harvest and thresh the wheat simultaneously, thus dispensing with the triple operations of harvesting, shocking and threshing the grain in vogue around 1900. The time lag between harvesting and threshing under the old method sometimes amounted to two or three weeks; today, there is no interval at all.

By making some minor adjustments, the combine can be used for the dual purposes of picking and shelling corn and harvesting and threshing wheat.

The best wheat produces up to 80 bushels per acre; a combine can harvest and thresh 50 acres of wheat in one day, if the wheat is good and the weather is favorable.

The percentage of the total population engaged in agriculture was 90 percent in 1790, 72 percent in 1820, 64 percent in 1850, 49 percent in 1880, 39 percent in 1900, 27 percent in 1920, 12 percent in 1950 and is less than 5 percent today. It is apparent that the most pronounced changes took place as a result of the mechanization of agriculture beginning in the 1830s and again in the 1920s.

Most farm families now own an automobile or so, truck, telephone, television, inside toilet facilities, electric or gas cooking stove, central heat, electric lights, washing machine, refrigerator, deep freeze and other comforts of urban life. Few cows are kept for milk and butter; but the garden and the orchard still furnish vegetables and fruit for the table. Grocery stores are patronized by the farm women to an extent unheard of sixty to seventy years ago. It is not unusual for a typical farmer to own—along with the bank—a quarter of a million dollars' worth of farm equipment and land.

Community log rollings, hog killings and wheat threshings have passed with the horse and buggy days. Village baseball games, coon hunts, country dances, shivarees, and other old-time pastimes have almost entirely disappeared. The automobile has extended the horizon of the farmer from only a few miles at the turn of the century to the entire country today.

An equally revolutionary change has taken place in the public schools. The one-room, one-teacher elementary schools and the half-dozen high schools scattered over the county seventy years ago have given way to a modern system. Some consolidation took place over the past few decades; but the present plan is the result of a survey made by Purdue University in 1956. Purdue recommended that the county be divided into two metropolitan school districts, with headquarters at Mt. Vernon in the south and Poseyville in the north. However, Harmony Township refused to join and still maintains its own township system with headquarters in New Harmony.

A senior and a junior high school are located at each of the three headquarters. In addition, elementary schools are conveniently situated throughout the districts. The school grounds are large. The buildings are modern and commodious. The high schools have auditoriums, band, music, television and drafting rooms, print, mechanic and farm shops, libraries, kitchens and cafeterias. Pupils are carried to and from school in busses. About seventy-five percent of them graduate from high school, and about thirty percent go to college.

Beginning teachers are required to have a bachelor's degree and high school teachers a master's degree. Salaries range from around $9,000 to $12,000 per year—a tremendous increase over the $320 per year paid to beginning teachers at the turn of the century for teaching all the first eight grades.

No other type of building so becomes a landscape as the white, one-story, frame country church with its facade-end steeple pointing toward the sky. The beauty and the serenity of a country church in a setting of trees casts a spell over one as he gazes upon it and contemplates the part it has played in country life. Some of these churches still deck the countryside; others have been abandoned; while a few have been rebuilt with brick.

Unfortunately, the country church has lost its importance, not only for its original religious functions but also as a social gathering place for farmers and their wives. Attendance now is at a low ebb. The automobile, the radio and the television now provide the news, the entertainment, and the escape from isolation of country life which country churches earlier furnished.

Posey County has benefited economically from the discovery of oil and gas and the great increase in the per acre production of corn and wheat. The farmers have been the chief beneficiaries of most of this new wealth. Mt. Vernon, too, has prospered through the acquisition of an oil refinery, small manufacturing businesses, and a $25,000,000 plant for the fabrication of heavywall pressure vessels for nuclear power stations and petrochemical plants.

The public roads, though, are hardly in keeping with the general prosperity of the county. Roads connecting the principal towns are two-lane, hard-top highways; but most of the auxiliary ones are second- or third-grade with only a covering of loose gravel. The Old Plank Road between New Harmony and Mt. Vernon has been marked with historical tablets near the approaches of these two towns. The old covered bridge at Solitude has gone with the wind, and so have the other covered bridges.

CHAPTER EIGHTEEN

National Historical Monuments

NEW HARMONY

NEW HARMONY IS still a small country village of 1,000 residents, about the same size as it was around the turn of the century. Its historical importance was recognized officially during its sesquicentennial year of 1964. It was dedicated a National Historical Landmark in commemoration of its founding by the Harmonists in 1814 and its flowering under the Owenites, who succeeded them in 1825. The Secretary of the Interior made the presentation of the award to the Governor of Indiana, who accepted it on behalf of the people of the State. The ceremony was attended by a galaxy of educators, writers, publishers, directors of art galleries and museums, politicians and other notables from throughout the United States and abroad. This celebration would have astonished the town's citizens who had lived there in earlier days.

Most of the buildings of the Harmonists have withstood the ravages of time, a fine testimonial to the craftsmanship of the early artisans, despite the handicaps and hardships of pioneer days. Many of their thirty-four two-story residences are still used as homes. Other principal landmarks are the Brick Dormitory originally occupied by the Rappite men, Poet's House, Harmonist House, Log House, Fauntleroy Home, Fort-Granary, and Burial Ground without tombstones.

Buildings of the Owenites still standing are Owen Laboratory, built by David Dale Owen and used in making the geological surveys of the northwest areas; Rapp-Maclure Mansion, lived in from time to time by prominent Harmonists; Barret Gate House, which incorporates the Log House built by the Harmonists; and the Workingman's Institute and Library founded by Maclure.

The Owenites used the Harmonist dormitory as the first public school in America. It is now a museum. The frame house built by the Harmonists was renamed the Fauntleroy Home, and in 1859 it became the birthplace of the first women's club in the United States with a written constitution. It, too, is a museum. A formal garden was constructed by the Harmonists. The original was replaced by a new one in 1939. It was a labyrinth of concentric rings of narrow trimmed hedge with narrow paths between. It had more than one entrance. The quest was to select the one which led to the center of the labyrinth. The intricate green maze is symbolic of the options open to an individual during his lifetime and the reward awaiting him at the end of his days, depending upon whether he makes the right choice or the wrong one.

One of the most beautiful contributions made by the Owenites are the golden rain trees. Their beauty is evident throughout the entire year—in the spring by their fern-like, serrated, dark-green leaves; in the summer by their profuse, terminal clusters of golden blossoms that drop in yellow showers and give the trees their poetic name; in the fall by their multi-colored, air-tight seeded pods about the size of a lime and the shape of a Japanese lantern; and in winter by their bare, symmetrical limbs.*

A great deal has been done during the past few years to preserve the old landmarks of the Harmonists and Owenites. The Indiana Department of National Resources, National Society of Colonial Dames of America, and Robert Lee Blaffer Trust have all participated in this worthwhile undertaking. The Blaffer Trust was founded by Jane Blaffer Owen, who married Kenneth D. Owen, a great-grandson of Richard Owen and a great-great-grandson of Robert Owen.

A celebration of the founding of Purdue University one hundred

---

*From Blair's *The New Harmony Story,* pp. 60–62. Used with permission.

years ago was held in New Harmony in 1969, at which Dr. F. L. Hovde, the President of Purdue University, gave unstinted praise to Richard Owen as educator, scientist, soldier and first President of Purdue. He presented a plaque dedicated by the alumni to the Purdue Centennial Year, which was to be placed on the Rapp-Maclure Home.

Despite New Harmony's pride in the past, it went modern to some extent in 1961 when the Robert Lee Blaffer Trust built a non-denominational roofless church in the shape of a towering dome. The idea was inspired by a remark attributed to George Sand that only the sky is vast enough to shelter all worshipping humanity. Architect Philip Johnson designed the church, and it received the First Honor Award of the American Institute of Architects in 1961.

The horizontal plan consists of seven equal interlocking circles. One is on the granite paving-block floor in the center of the church and defined by a circular stone wall. The other six are parabolically curved and conterminously arranged to form the outer wall. The frame is made of laminated pinewood beams and covered on the outside with split shake shingles. The entire structure is supported by six ponderous monoliths of Indiana limestone, with high, open intervening arches, permitting entrance from any direction. The dome rises upward about fifty feet, tapering inwardly. The diameter at the vertex is about one-third as great as it is at the base.

The shape and the material used in its construction give the church the appearance of an inverted rosebud and its shadow the semblance of a full-blown rose. The form was inspired by the prophecy of Micah foretelling the coming of the millenium: "Unto thee shall come a golden rose," which the Harmonists believed was just around the corner.

A semi-open, heart-shaped bronze statue by the sculptor Jacques Lipchitz, standing in the inner circle of the church, is its only ornament. A seraphim and a cherubim support it, a symbolic Lamb of God faces it, and a dove hovers overhead. The statue is variously referred to as "The Madonna of the Inverted Heart," "The Descent of the Holy Spirit," "The Incarnation," and "The Virgin."

125

The setting of the roofless church enhances its beauty. It is built inside a large court enclosed by a red-rose, sandmold brick wall, with sculptured bronze gates designed by Lipchitz, and paved with limestone blocks. Yew, spruce and golden rain trees inside the court and Japanese crab apple and haw trees outside the wall make a decorative frame for the church.

The open roof, reminiscent of the Pantheon of Rome, the high open arches between the monoliths at the base, and the lone bronze statue in the inner circle give the impression that the church is open to all humanity. A fitting memorial to the Utopias of the Harmonists and the Owenites that flourished in New Harmony!

Another modern addition to New Harmony is the Paul Tillich Park, where the famous theologian lies buried. It is studded with Norwegian spruce, and some of Tillich's best-known sayings are carved on rocks set in strategic places throughout the park.*

Recently, there has been an enormous increase in restoration of old buildings of the Harmonists and Owenites and construction of new ones. The plan is to spend more that $21,000,000, amounting to about $22,000 for each resident. The Lilly Endowment Foundation of Indianapolis joined the other benefactors and agreed to contribute almost $6,000,000 to the project.

In addition to the work of restoration, new buildings—inn, hotel, motel, clinic, hospital, and atheneum—are either completed or under construction inside the village. The atheneum is a museum and educational facility with an ampitheater containing 1,000 seats.

Outside the limits of New Harmony, the State of Indiana has acquired land for a state park with a three-mile front along the Wabash; and developers are building two subdivisions of new homes.

This new activity has created new jobs, and commercial rentals in the two-block business section have increased about 1500 percent during the past three years.

The American Academy of Arts and Sciences already sponsors symposiums on various topics. A number of universities conduct

*The information regarding the roofless church and the Paul Tillich Park is found in Blair's *The New Harmony Story,* pp. 63–65, 70, and is used with permission.

classes in weaving, pottery-making, archeology, stage-craft, drama, ballet and film for nine-month courses. Theatrical and musical programs are held in the theatres.

All persons interested in New Harmony are proud of its past and are hoping to revive an interest in the culture of its early halcyon days. Statesmen, educators, churchmen, musicians, artists, architects, editors, lecturers, biographers, and officials of museums and art galleries have come from various parts of the United States and from abroad to imbibe some of the culture and history of the town's heyday, and its unique spirit of confidence in the rationality of man. One architect made a trip from France for the sole purpose of seeing the modern roofless church. The Secretary of the Smithsonian Institution was one of the visitors, a well-deserved tribute to Robert Dale Owen, who introduced the bill for the creation of the Smithsonian Institution and was one of its first regents.

It is hoped that 500,000 or more tourists will eventually visit New Harmony annually to imbibe some of the culture of the communistic, religious and educational theories of the Harmonists and the Owenites, when they lived on the banks of the Wabash during the early decades of the nineteenth century.*

LINCOLN'S INDIANA HOME

In 1963, the old farm near Gentryville on which Thomas Lincoln staked his claim in 1816 was dedicated as the "Lincoln Boyhood National Memorial" in commemoration of the fourteen years that Abraham lived there. A considerable part of the ground is covered with scaly bark hickories and other hardwood trees. Trails lead through the woodsy terrain between the site of the Lincoln log cabin, the cemetery, and Gentryville about a mile away. Considerately, it has been decided to do as little modernizing as possible to the area.

*For recent stories regarding New Harmony's Restoration, see *Louisville Courier Magazine,* July 14, 1963; *Louisville Courier Journal,* July 24, 1974; *Medical News Magazine,* May, 1976; *New York Times,* October 11, 1975; *The News Sentinel,* Fort Wayne, July 3, 1976; *Wall Street Journal,* December 30, 1975; *Signature Magazine,* February, 1976.

A two-winged memorial building, constructed of Indiana limestone, has been dedicated to Abraham and his mother, Nancy Hanks. It is situated in a setting of trees and contains the Abraham Lincoln Chapel with a wainscot of cherry wood, the Nancy Hanks Lincoln Hall with a landscape painting of the place where the Lincolns crossed the Ohio River on their way to their new Indiana home, a museum, and historical data of Lincoln's life.

Panels on the outside walls within the court depict Lincoln's Kentucky and Indiana homes; and his receiving congratulations of his election to Congress in 1846, emancipating the slaves in 1863, and conferring with General Grant after his victory over General Lee.

A plaza occupies the space immediately north of the Memorial Building, and an alley leads up a gentle slope to the cemetery at the top of the knoll where Nancy Hanks and other early pioneers lie buried.

One may walk over the trail from the cemetery to the site of the Lincoln log cabin several hundred yards beyond. Alongside the trail is a cornfield, which presumably Thomas and Abraham cleared shortly after moving from Kentucky.

The site of the log cabin is marked by sills, hearth and fireplace made of bronze and enclosed with a stone wall. Hard by is a worm fence, reminiscent of the rails Abraham split during his boyhood days.

In addition to the original Lincoln homesite, there are a reconstructed log cabin, barn, barnyard, corncrib, chicken house, crafts shop, tools and crops, similar to those of Lincoln's time in Indiana.

The State of Indiana established the Lincoln State Park in memory of Lincoln in 1932. It is south of and coterminous with the Lincoln Boyhood National Memorial. Within the park is the Little Pigeon Primitive Church built on the side of the old log cabin in which the Lincoln family worshipped. Abraham's sister, Sarah Lincoln Grisby, and other early pioneers lie buried in its church-yard.

Thousands of visitors visit the Lincoln Boyhood National

Memorial and the Lincoln State Park annually, to reflect upon the immortal statements of the Emancipator and to hike along the trails, cast for game fish in the well-stocked, eighty-five-acre artificial lake, camp in the woods, and drive along the well-paved roads.

In nearby Rockport the Lincoln Pioneer Village in City Park is a memorial to Lincoln's sojourn near Gentryville, now called Lincoln City. It contains the Gentry Mansion in memory of James Gentry, who employed Lincoln and allegedly paid him twenty-five cents a day; the office of John Pitcher, the lawyer, from whom Lincoln borrowed law books to read and who interested him in the law; a museum of early transportation; and a replica of the Old Pigeon Baptist Church, which Lincoln helped to build but which he did not join.

CHAPTER NINETEEN

Country Life Around the Year 2000

ON MY RETURN to Washington from my pilgrimage to the banks of the Wabash and Ohio, my friend was anxious to have my reaction to the changes I noticed in country life since the beginning of the century.

"The most important ones have been the mechanization of agriculture and the consolidation of the country schools," was my reply. "The tractor has lifted the age-old burden of tilling the soil from the backs of the farmers and rendered the horse and mule obsolete. The automobile has extended the horizon of the farmers from the farm to the Atlantic and Pacific. The consolidation of the schools has provided country children educational opportunities comparable to those of children in cities and towns."

"Despite these improvements, there must be some drawbacks," my friend demurred.

"Naturally. I heard a great deal of longing for the 'good old days,' especially among the old-timers. They say that there is no romance in the tractor; that no longer can a farmer give Old Dobbin an affectionate pat on his neck, and have him acknowledge by rubbing his nose against the farmer's hand."

"Presumably, the old-timers were your contemporaries during the early days on the farm?"

"Not all, as most of them have gone to their reward. A number of my pupils at Downen School around the turn of the century were still on the farms. They have progressed with the times, and some have become beneficiaries of the discovery of oil and gas, and the enormous increase in the productivity of their land."

"And what about the young folk on the farms today?"

"The rural mirth and charms of country life of yesterday are gone. The disciplines of life are very much relaxed, as there is no longer much need for them. On the whole, however, I would say that most young people living on the farms are doing what is right. One does not find the dissatisfaction and the dissension that prevails in the cities today, although a number of young people living on the farms also work in town."

"How about the consolidation of the schools?" asked my friend.

"Some people complain about the long hours the children have to ride the busses, going to and from school, sometimes an hour each way. In the winter time, they leave shortly after daylight and do not return home until dark."

"Does the farmer have a much easier life today than at the turn of the century?"

"His work is certainly much less onerous; however, sometimes his hours are longer and his work is more humdrum. Some farmers are "moonlighters," so called, because they work in town during the daytime and do their farming on weekends and at night, using modern tractors with shockproof lights."

"A farmer should feel gratified with being able to accomplish as much as twenty-five or even fifty men could do around 1900," my friend remarked.

"True, incredible progress has been made in agriculture since I worked on the farm, but nothing compared with what is in store for the dawn of the next century, according to the prognostications from the Department of Agriculture. Present farming methods will be as antiquated in the year 2,000 as those of 1900 are obsolete today. The farmer will be freed even from the arduous labor of cultivating the soil, planting and harvesting the crops; he will have more leisure for recreation, entertainment, and advanced learning; and his children will enjoy educational opportunities unheard of today."

"How do they expect such Utopian dreams to be realized?"

131

"The farmer will sit in his air-conditioned farm office, scan a print-out from a computer center, type out an inquiry on a keyboard, which will relay his question to the computer center. The latter will transmit the inquiry to a satellite equipped with the most sophisticated, remote-sensing instruments. It will send back information as to the condition of the soil, the number of acres to plant, the time to sow, the types of seeds and fertilizer to use. Crops will then be planted scientifically. Later in the season, the sensor will advise the farmer when the crop is ready for harvesting."

"That sounds more like fancy than reality," said my skeptical friend.

"But the soothsayers do not stop here. They say that the preparation of the soil, the planting, the cultivating, and the harvesting will be done by automatic machinery directed by tape recorders and supervised by television scanners mounted on towers. High-speed robot harvesters will pick, grade and package the crop and deliver it to transportation depots for distribution to retail warehouses. They say that farmers will work one-third fewer hours; that the demand for recreation will be three times as great; and that the number of automobiles will increase twofold."

"I must say, it is difficult to go along with such visionaries," my friend said, shaking his head dubiously.

"The experts say there will be long-range forecasting of the weather, so that heavy rains, snow and windstorms can be foretold in time to divert or at least minimize damage."

"Apparently, the only thing left for the farmer to do will be to mow the lawn and trim the hedge around the yard, now and then, when he is not sitting on the front porch taking it easy."

"You underestimate the crystal gazers! He will be able to control the height of the lawn grass and the growth of the hedge by using artificial lights and growth-regulating chemicals, so that mowing and trimming will no longer be necessary. By these same means, farmers will be able to shorten or lengthen the time required for the ripening of their crops in accordance with advice received from the satellite sensor. Hence, it will be possible to accelerate the maturity of the crops in one part of the country and retard it in another. In this way they will be ready for marketing at the most favorable time."

"Any more fanciful predictions?"

"Weeds will become mere laboratory curiosities. Mosquitoes, flies, and other insects will be a thing of the past. The fly swatter will be a museum-piece."

"How do the prognosticators expect that to be brought about?"

"By the application of biological and chemical substances."

"Where will that leave the birds, with no bugs or worms to eat?"

"I suppose the birds will have to live on frozen foods, which the experts say will be the fate of the human race, too, around 2,000."

"Are these predictions made seriously or out of Jules Verne?"

"As serious prognostications. Fires caused by lightning will be curtailed; trees will be tailor-made as to sex, height, and other characteristics; parasite and predator damage will be controlled; the land will present a striped pattern caused by separating the rows of the crops with impervious strips to catch the rainfall and drain it to nourish the plants. Whole hillsides which are unproductive today will be prepared to shed previously wasted rainfull and deliver it into reservoirs and small lakes to serve towns and recreation areas. Reservoirs and lakes will be treated to prevent evaporation."

"It always has been my understanding that rainfall came from evaporated water. What will be its source, if evaporation is stopped?"

"I imagine from evaporation from the untreated large lakes, rivers, and the ocean. The predictors did say that irrigation would be automated and controlled by computers; that the water used for irrigation would be from poor-quality sources; and that fresh water would be used for domestic and recreation purposes alone, to save energy in pumping it."

"It seems to me that these predictions should be taken with a big grain of salt."

"Perhaps that is true; but you have not heard everything. The agriculture experts say that livestock will be grown for market on two-thirds of the feed in two-thirds of the time required today. Cornstalks will grow multiple ears and cotton plants will produce bolls clustered on top for easy picking; crops will need only a fraction of the water required today; droughts will have very little effect; plants will grow and mature much faster.''

"I should think that all of these so-called advantages would take the joy out of the farmer's life and destroy the intimacy between man and his land."

"I agree with you. Moreover, there will be fewer farmers around the year 2,000, one out of 100 of the population, compared with less than five today. The high costs of agricultural implements already has driven many farmers to the wall. The experts admit that the costs of automated equipment at the dawn of the next century will be in the tens of thousands instead of thousands of dollars today. The government, they say, will furnish the credit, which means that the government will control agriculture even more than it does today."

"When still another four percent of the people are driven from the farms, where will they go?"

"If the experts are correct, thousands of new towns will spring up throughout the countrysides in which the dislocated farmers as well as the city unemployed will live; factories will be moved from congested areas and new ones will be built in the neighborhoods of the new cities and towns, to avoid the tremendous waste of time and energy now spent on commuting by auto over the crowded freeways."

"It seems to me that the theory of agriculture overlooks the devastating effect of automation in industry up to the present time. Will there be more jobs in factories merely because they are scattered throughout the United States?"

"Only time will tell."

"There is one thing we can agree upon, without any doubt. The good old days are gone forever," said my friend, with a wistful note in his voice.

"Yes, 'the tender grace of the days that are gone' has passed like a shadow before the sun."*

---

*The ideas advanced above were taken from the addresses of the Secretary of Agriculture, published on or about June, 1967, by the United States Department of Agriculture under the title *Agriculture/2000.*